100
ground beef dishes
from 1 easy recipe

100

ground beef
dishes

from 1 easy recipe

This edition published in 2011

LOVE FOOD is an imprint of Parragon Books Ltd

Parragon
Chartist House
15-17 Trim Street
Bath BA1 1HA, UK

Copyright © Parragon Books Ltd 2010

LOVE FOOD and the accompanying heart device is a registered
trade mark of Parragon Books Ltd in Australia, the UK, USA, India,
and the EU.

www.parragon.com

ISBN: 978-1-4454-6258-5

Printed in China

Cover design by Talking Design
Written by Linda Doeser
Internal design by Simon Levy
Photography by Clive Bozzard-Hill
Home economy by Valerie Barrett

Notes for the Reader
This book uses standard kitchen measuring spoons and cups. All
spoon and cup measurements are level unless otherwise indicated.
Unless otherwise stated, milk is assumed to be whole, eggs are
large, individual vegetables are medium, and pepper is freshly
ground black pepper.

The times given are only an approximate guide. Preparation times
differ according to the techniques used by different people and the
cooking times may also vary from those given. Optional ingredients,
variations, or serving suggestions have not been included in the
calculations.

Recipes using raw or very lightly cooked eggs should be avoided
by infants, the elderly, pregnant women, convalescents, and anyone
with a chronic illness. Pregnant and breast-feeding women are
advised to avoid eating peanuts and peanut products. People with
nut allergies should be aware that some of the prepared ingredients
used in the recipes in this book may contain nuts. Always check the
packaging before use.

Contents

6 Introduction

12 Easy

56 Favorite

94 Comforting

140 Spicy

184 Special

222 Index

Introduction

One of the best things about ground beef is its versatility. It goes with a vast range of ingredients to create a wide variety of different meals from hamburgers to pasta sauces and from stuffed vegetables to pastry turnovers. Its most immediately obvious partners are onions and garlic and, perhaps, tomatoes, mushrooms, and herbs, but it responds to a multitude of flavors and textures, whether hot or aromatic spices, peas and beans, many kinds of cheese, a huge array of vegetables, and a lot of sauces and condiments, from soy sauce to mustard. Perhaps surprisingly, it even combines well with fruit, such as apples and raisins.

As a general rule, the basic ground beef mix (see page 10) works in one of two ways. The raw ingredients can be mixed together until thoroughly combined and then shaped into meatballs, hamburgers, dumplings, kabobs, croquettes, or meatloaf before cooking. Alternatively, the various ingredients can be cooked in a pan or casserole so that the flavors mingle deliciously for pasta sauces, casseroles, stews, gratins, and even soups. However, there are still many more variations—all kinds of wraps from omelets to tortillas, puffs, fritters, and muffins, baked and layered dishes, and unusual meat and vegetable rolls.

Quality & Economy

Ground beef is undoubtedly an economical choice for family meals, not least because a little can go a long way. This is especially true when it is combined with other ingredients, such as breadcrumbs, to make meatballs or hamburgers, or when it is served with plenty of filling carbohydrate, such as pasta or a topping of mashed potatoes. It is easy to cook—in the following pages there are 100 easy-to-follow tasty recipes for all occasions—and it is popular with adults and children alike.

However, the quality of ground beef can vary widely and buying the cheapest you can find may often prove to be a false economy. Many grocery stores sell "bargain" packages and although the meat may look perfectly satisfactory, it usually contains quite a high percentage of fat. Not only is this less healthy, it is also wasteful. In the long run, meat labeled "chuck" is an economical choice with a reasonable amount of fat and has a better flavor. "Ground round" and "ground sirloin" are leaner cuts, but they can become too dry for hamburgers and are a better choice where other ingredients are added, such as in meatballs and meat loaf.

Ground beef doesn't keep for long in the refrigerator, but raw meat can be frozen for up to three months. Many cooked dishes, such as Bolognese sauce, also freeze well, so batch cooking is a good way to save both money and time.

When buying ground beef, check the expiration date and make sure that the package isn't damaged and is properly sealed. Store on a low shelf in the refrigerator, away from cooked foods and ingredients intended to be eaten raw. If the package is damaged or you have bought it loose from the butcher, remove the packaging, transfer the meat to a covered dish, and store in the refrigerator. Ideally, ground beef should be cooked and eaten on the day of purchase.

Ground beef will always contain some fat. This is why it is easy to brown in a nonstick pan without adding any oil—a technique that is the perfect start for many recipes. For some recipes, it is very important to drain off as much fat as possible after browning the meat—with or without additional oil—as the mixture needs to be quite dry. In fact, it is always worth checking the pan after browning ground beef and, if it does look a little greasy, draining off the excess.

Equipment

All the recipes in this book can be prepared and cooked with the tools and equipment found in most kitchens—measuring cups, cutting boards, knives, pans and skillets, mixing bowls, and so on. The only specialty pan suggested in one or two recipes is a wok—a large pan with sloping sides designed for stir-frying—but you can use a skillet instead, although it is not quite so easy to keep the ingredients moving while they cook.

It is worth buying the best-quality pans you can afford and, if you look after them well, they will last many years. A pan with a thick, solid bottom, preferably ground flat rather than stamped flat, distributes heat well so that the food cooks evenly. Make sure that the handles are secure and lids fit tightly. Always use the correct-size pan because one that is too small may cause ingredients to cook unevenly or boil

over, while one that is too large may result in the dish drying out. A flameproof casserole is extremely useful and can double as a large pan.

It is also worth buying good-quality knives and an efficient sharpener. Keep knives sharp, because not only are they more efficient when sharp, but they are also much safer. Blunt knives can easily slip and cut your hand. Store them in a knife block or a wall-mounted magnetic rack out of the reach of children. Do not store them in a drawer where other tools may damage the cutting edges. Always use a wooden or plastic cutting board when slicing or dicing, because hard materials, such as glass, metal, or granite, can damage the blades.

About the Basic Ground Beef Mix

As ground beef is so versatile, the basic ground beef mix is very flexible and easily adapted. Onions always feature, but in some recipes a different member of the onion family, such as shallots or scallions, is substituted. Garlic is a valuable addition in many dishes, but it is optional because some people find its flavor too pungent.

Herbs, spices, and flavorings are added to the basic mix to give each dish its unique character, and quantities vary from a pinch to several tablespoons, depending on the strength of flavor. A huge range features throughout the book—fresh and dried herbs, hot and aromatic spices, sauces and condiments, fresh and dried chiles, to name just a few. Other ingredients, such as stock, canned or fresh tomatoes, potatoes, breadcrumbs, and mushrooms, vary according to the type of dish.

Basic Ground Beef Mix

Serves 4–6

- ✳ 2 lb 4 oz/1 kg ground beef
- ✳ 1 onion, finely chopped (recipes may substitute Bermuda onions, red onions, shallots, or scallions)
- ✳ 1 garlic clove, finely chopped (optional)
- ✳ salt and pepper

This is the basic mix that all 100 variations of ground beef dishes in the book are based on.

For each recipe, the basic mix is highlighted (✳) for easy reference, so then all you have to do is follow the easy steps each time and a world of delicious and tempting meals will await you.

Please note that the ingredient quantities vary from time to time so please check these carefully.

Easy

Beef & Tomato Soup

1. Heat the oil in a large pan. Add the onion and garlic and cook over low heat, stirring occasionally, for 5 minutes, until softened. Stir in the chiles and tomatoes and cook for an additional 5 minutes. Add the ground beef, increase the heat to medium, and cook, breaking it up with a wooden spoon, for 6–8 minutes, until lightly browned.

2. Stir in the carrots, potatoes, and parsley, pour in the stock, and season to taste with salt and pepper. Bring to a boil, then reduce the heat, cover, and simmer for 30 minutes, until the meat and vegetables are tender.

3. Taste and adjust the seasoning, adding salt and pepper if needed. Ladle the soup into warmed bowls, garnish with parsley, and serve immediately with crusty rolls.

Serves 6

3 tbsp sunflower oil

1 onion, finely chopped

1 garlic clove, finely chopped

2 fresh red chiles, seeded and finely chopped

4 large tomatoes, peeled and chopped

1 lb 2 oz/500 g ground beef

2 carrots, diced

2 potatoes, diced

1–2 tbsp chopped fresh flat-leaf parsley, plus extra to garnish

5 cups beef stock

salt and pepper

crusty rolls, to serve

Homemade Hamburgers

1. Put the ground beef, onion, parsley, and Worcestershire sauce into a bowl, season to taste with salt and pepper, and mix well with your hands until thoroughly combined.

2. Divide the mixture into 6 equal-size portions and shape each into a ball, then gently flatten into a hamburger shape. If you have time, chill in the refrigerator for 30 minutes to firm up.

3. Heat the oil in a large skillet. Add the hamburgers, in batches, and cook over medium heat for 5–8 minutes on each side, turning them carefully with a spatula. Remove from the skillet and keep warm while you cook the remaining hamburgers.

4. Serve in toasted hamburger buns with lettuce leaves, tomato slices, dill pickles, and ketchup.

Serves 6

* 2 lb 4 oz/1 kg ground beef
* 1 small onion, grated
  1 tbsp chopped fresh parsley
  2 tsp Worcestershire sauce
  2 tbsp sunflower oil
* salt and pepper

To serve
6 hamburger buns, split and toasted
lettuce leaves
tomato slices
dill pickles, sliced
ketchup

Bacon Burgers

1. Preheat the broiler. Put the ground beef, onion, garlic (if using), breadcrumbs, sage, and egg into a bowl, season to taste with salt and pepper, and mix well until thoroughly combined. Divide the mixture into 6 equal-size portions and shape each into a ball, then gently flatten into a hamburger shape.

2. Wrap a bacon slice around each hamburger and secure with a wooden toothpick.

3. Brush one side of each hamburger with a little of the melted butter and cook under the preheated broiler for 5 minutes. Carefully turn the hamburgers with a spatula, brush with the remaining melted butter, and cook for an additional 4–5 minutes, until cooked to your liking.

4. Carefully transfer the hamburgers to warmed individual plates, remove the toothpicks, and serve immediately.

Serves 6

* 1 lb 7 oz/650 g ground beef
* 1 large onion, very finely chopped
* 1 garlic clove, very finely chopped (optional)
  1½ cups fresh breadcrumbs
  2 tsp chopped fresh sage
  1 extra large egg, lightly beaten
  6 bacon slices
  3 tbsp melted butter
* salt and pepper

Beef Keftas

1. Put the ground beef, onion, garlic, cilantro, and spices into a bowl and season to taste with salt and pepper. Add the egg and mix well with your hands until thoroughly combined and very smooth. Cover the bowl with plastic wrap and chill in the refrigerator for 30 minutes.

2. Meanwhile, combine the chopped mint and the yogurt in a bowl and season to taste with salt. Cover with plastic wrap and chill until required.

3. Preheat the broiler or barbecue. Remove the ground beef mixture from the refrigerator, scoop up pieces with your hands, and shape into small ovals about ¾ inch/2 cm thick. Thread the keftas onto metal or presoaked wooden skewers with 3 to each skewer.

4. Brush the broiler rack or barbecue grill with oil. Cook the skewers, in batches if necessary, under the preheated broiler or on the barbecue, turning occasionally, for 10–12 minutes, until cooked through. Garnish with mint leaves and lime wedges and serve immediately with the minted yogurt.

Serves 6–8

* 2 lb 4 oz/1 kg ground beef
* 1 Bermuda onion, grated
* 3 garlic cloves, very finely chopped
* 4 tbsp chopped fresh cilantro
* 1 tsp ground cumin
* ½ tsp ground cinnamon
* ½ tsp ground turmeric
* 1 tsp paprika
* 1 extra large egg, lightly beaten
* 3 tbsp finely chopped fresh mint, plus extra leaves to garnish
* ⅔ cup plain yogurt
* sunflower oil, for brushing
* salt and pepper
* lime wedges, to garnish

Beef with Scrambled Eggs

1. Melt the butter in a large pan. Add the onion and garlic and cook over low heat, stirring occasionally, for 5 minutes, until softened. Add the ground beef, increase the heat to medium, and cook, stirring frequently and breaking it up with a wooden spoon, for 8–10 minutes, until evenly browned.

2. Add the tomatoes and bell peppers, reduce the heat, and simmer, stirring occasionally, for 15 minutes, until the meat and vegetables are tender. Stir in the Worcestershire sauce and parsley and season to taste with salt and pepper.

3. Lightly beat the eggs in a bowl and season to taste with salt and pepper. Add the eggs to the pan and cook, stirring, for a few minutes, until lightly scrambled.

4. Garnish with parsley and serve immediately with toast.

Serves 6

6 tbsp butter

1 onion, sliced

1 garlic clove, finely chopped

1 lb 2 oz/500 g ground beef

2 tomatoes, peeled and sliced

1 small red bell pepper, seeded and diced

1 small yellow bell pepper, seeded and diced

1 tbsp Worcestershire sauce

1 tbsp chopped fresh parsley, plus extra to garnish

6 eggs

salt and pepper

buttered toast, to serve

Stir-Fried Beef

1. Combine half the rice wine, the garlic, ginger, soy sauce, sesame oil, and cornstarch in a bowl. Add the ground beef, turning and stirring to coat, cover with plastic wrap, and let marinate in the refrigerator for 1 hour.

2. Heat a wok over medium heat, then add the peanut oil, swirl it around the wok, and heat Remove the ground beef from the bowl, add it to the wok, and stir-fry, breaking it up with a wooden spoon, for 3–5 minutes, until evenly browned.

3. Stir in the remaining rice wine, the hoisin and oyster sauces, and rice vinegar and cook, stirring constantly, for 1 minute.

4. Stir in the carrots, scallions, broccoli, bell pepper, and baby corn and stir-fry for an additional 3–4 minutes, until the vegetables are tender-crisp. Serve immediately.

Serves 6

6 tbsp Chinese rice wine or dry sherry

3 garlic cloves, very finely chopped

2 tbsp finely chopped fresh ginger

1 tbsp dark soy sauce

1 tsp sesame oil

1 tbsp cornstarch

2 lb/900 g ground beef

3 tbsp peanut oil

2 tbsp hoisin sauce

2 tbsp oyster sauce

2 tsp rice vinegar

2 carrots, thinly sliced diagonally

4 scallions, thinly sliced lengthwise

2 cups broccoli florets

1 large red bell pepper, seeded and thinly sliced

1½ cups baby corn, halved lengthwise

Beef & Noodles

1. Cook the noodles according to the package directions, then drain and refresh under cold running water. Put them into a bowl, add 1 tablespoon of the sesame oil, and toss to coat.

2. Heat a wok over medium heat, then add the peanut oil, swirl it around the wok, and heat. Add the onion and stir-fry for a few minutes, until softened. Add the ground beef and stir-fry, breaking it up with a wooden spoon, for 3–5 minutes, until evenly browned.

3. Stir in the ginger, chile, and Chinese five-spice powder and cook, stirring constantly, for 1 minute, then add the carrots, bell pepper, and snow peas. Stir-fry for an additional 4 minutes.

4. Add the bean sprouts, the remaining sesame oil, and the noodles and stir-fry for an additional 2 minutes. Serve immediately.

Serves 6

1 lb/450 g dried egg noodles

2 tbsp sesame oil

2 tbsp peanut oil

1 onion, finely chopped

1 lb 7 oz/650 g ground beef

1-inch/2.5-cm piece fresh ginger, thinly sliced

1 fresh red chile, seeded and thinly sliced

1½ tsp Chinese five-spice powder

2 carrots, thinly sliced diagonally

1 red bell pepper, seeded and diced

1 cup snow peas

3 cups fresh bean sprouts

Beef Fried Rice

1. Cook the rice in a large pan of salted boiling water for 15 minutes, until tender. Drain the rice, rinse with boiling water, and set aside.

2. Heat a wok over medium heat, then add the peanut oil, swirl it around the wok, and heat. Add the eggs and cook, stirring constantly, for 50–60 seconds, until set. Transfer to a dish and set aside.

3. Add the ground beef to the wok and stir-fry, breaking it up with a wooden spoon, for 4–5 minutes, until evenly browned. Stir in the onion, garlic, and peas and stir-fry for an additional 3–4 minutes.

4. Add the rice, soy sauce, sugar, and eggs and cook, stirring constantly, for 1–2 minutes, until heated through. Serve immediately with shrimp chips.

Serves 6

2½ cups long-grain rice

2 tbsp peanut oil

4 extra large eggs, lightly beaten

1 lb 7 oz/650 g ground beef

1 large onion, finely chopped

2 garlic cloves, finely chopped

1¼ cups frozen peas

3 tbsp light soy sauce

1 tsp sugar

salt

shrimp chips, to serve

Quick Curry

1. Heat half the oil in a large pan. Add the onion, bell pepper, cumin seeds, cardamom pods, and bay leaves and cook over low heat, stirring constantly, for 2–3 minutes, until the spices give off their aroma. Add the tomatoes and cook, stirring frequently, for 10 minutes.

2. Meanwhile, heat the remaining oil in a skillet. Add the garlic and cook, stirring frequently, for 1 minute, then add the ground beef, coriander, turmeric, and chili powder. Cook over medium heat, stirring constantly and breaking up the meat with a wooden spoon, for 4–5 minutes, until the meat is evenly browned. Transfer the mixture to the pan with the tomatoes.

3. Pour in the stock and bring to a boil, then reduce the heat, cover, and simmer, stirring occasionally, for 20–25 minutes. If the mixture seems to be drying out, add a little water.

4. Remove and discard the bay leaves and cardamom pods, then season to taste with salt. Scatter over the cilantro and serve immediately with rice and naan.

Serves 4

4 tbsp peanut oil

1 large onion, finely chopped

1 green bell pepper, seeded and diced

1 tsp cumin seeds

4 green cardamom pods

2 bay leaves

1 lb 2 oz/500 g tomatoes, peeled and chopped

2 garlic cloves, finely chopped

1 lb/450 g ground beef

2 tsp ground coriander

2 tsp ground turmeric

1 tsp chili powder

2½ cups beef stock

2 tbsp chopped fresh cilantro

salt

cooked rice and naan, to serve

Thai Beef Omelet

1. Heat half the oil in a skillet. Add the scallions and garlic and cook over low heat, stirring occasionally, for 4–5 minutes, until softened. Add the ground beef, increase the heat to medium, and cook, stirring frequently and breaking it up with a wooden spoon, for 5–8 minutes, until evenly browned.

2. Stir in the tomatoes, chile, sugar, and 2 tablespoons of the fish sauce and season to taste with pepper. Reduce the heat and simmer, stirring occasionally, for 15–20 minutes, until thickened and cooked through. Stir in the chopped cilantro.

3. Beat the eggs with the remaining fish sauce in a bowl. Heat half the remaining oil in an omelet pan. Add half the egg mixture, tilt the pan to spread it evenly, and cook over low heat for a few minutes, until just set.

4. Spoon half the ground beef mixture into the center of the omelet. Using a spatula, fold in the sides to make a neat parcel and slide it out of the pan onto a warmed serving dish. Make a second omelet in the same way with the remaining oil, beaten egg, and ground beef mixture. Garnish with cilantro sprigs and serve immediately.

Serves 2

4 tbsp peanut oil

4 scallions, finely chopped

2 garlic cloves, finely chopped

8 oz/225 g ground beef

2 tomatoes, peeled and chopped

1 fresh red chile, seeded and finely chopped

1 tsp sugar

3 tbsp Thai fish sauce

1 tbsp chopped fresh cilantro, plus extra sprigs to garnish

6 eggs

pepper

Tex-Mex Pizza

1. Preheat the oven to 400°F/200°C. Brush a baking sheet with oil. Heat the oil in a pan. Add the onion and garlic and cook over low heat, stirring occasionally, for 5 minutes, until softened. Add the ground beef, increase the heat to medium, and cook, stirring frequently and breaking it up with a wooden spoon, for 5–8 minutes, until evenly browned.

2. Drain off any excess fat. Stir in the cumin, jalapeño chiles, and refried beans, pour in the water, and season to taste with salt. Reduce the heat and simmer gently for 5 minutes, then remove from the heat.

3. Meanwhile, make the pizza dough. Sift the flour and salt into a bowl. Add the butter, cut it into the dry ingredients, and rub in with your fingertips until the mixture resembles breadcrumbs. Pour in most of the milk and mix with a round-bladed knife to form a soft dough, adding the remaining milk if needed. Turn out the dough onto a lightly floured surface and knead gently. Roll out to a 10-inch/25-cm circle and transfer to the prepared baking sheet. Push up the edge slightly all around to make a rim.

4. Spread the ground beef mixture evenly over the pizza crust and sprinkle with the cheese. Bake in the preheated oven for 18–20 minutes, until the cheese has melted and is golden. Top with avocado slices, red chile slices, and sour cream. Serve immediately.

Serves 2

2 tbsp sunflower oil, plus extra for brushing

1 small onion, finely chopped

1 garlic clove, finely chopped

8 oz/225 g ground beef

1 tsp ground cumin

4 pickled jalapeño chiles, drained and finely chopped

14 oz/400 g canned refried beans

⅔ cup water

2¼ cups grated Monterey Jack or cheddar cheese

salt

Pizza dough
1½ cups self-rising flour, plus extra for dusting

pinch of salt

2 tbsp butter

½ cup milk

To garnish
avocado slices

fresh red chile slices

sour cream

Crispy Beef Fritters

1. Beat the egg yolks in a large bowl until pale and thick. Fold in the ground beef, onion, baking powder, parsley, and Worcestershire sauce and season to taste with salt and pepper. Stir gently until thoroughly combined.

2. Stiffly whisk the egg whites in a separate grease-free bowl, then gently fold them into the ground beef mixture.

3. Heat the oil in a large skillet. Drop tablespoonfuls of the ground beef mixture, about 4 at a time, into the hot oil and fry for 3 minutes, or until puffed up and brown at the edges. Using a spatula or slotted spoon, turn the fritters over and fry for an additional 2–3 minutes.

4. Remove with a slotted spoon and drain on paper towels. Keep warm while you cook the remaining batches, then serve immediately.

Serves 4

4 eggs, separated

8 oz/225 g ground beef

1 small onion, very finely chopped

½ tsp baking powder

2 tbsp chopped fresh parsley

1 tbsp Worcestershire sauce

4 tbsp sunflower oil

salt and pepper

One-Pot Pasta

1. Heat the oil in a large pan with a tight-fitting lid. Add the onion, garlic, celery, and carrot and cook over low heat, stirring occasionally, for 5 minutes, until softened. Add the ground beef, increase the heat to medium, and cook, stirring frequently and breaking it up with a wooden spoon, for 5–8 minutes, until evenly browned.

2. Add the mushrooms and cook for an additional 3–4 minutes. Add the tomatoes, tomato paste, sugar, herbs, pasta, and wine. Stir in the concentrated stock, add just enough water to cover, and stir well.

3. Reduce the heat, cover tightly, and simmer gently for 15–20 minutes, until the pasta is tender but still firm to the bite and the sauce has thickened. Season to taste with salt and pepper. Serve immediately.

Serves 4

2 tbsp olive oil

1 onion, chopped

1 garlic clove, finely chopped

1 celery stalk, chopped

1 carrot, chopped

1 lb 2 oz/500 g ground beef

1⅔ cups sliced mushrooms

14 oz/400 g canned chopped tomatoes

1 tbsp tomato paste

1 tsp sugar

pinch of dried oregano

1 tbsp chopped fresh flat-leaf parsley

6 oz/175 g dried fusilli

¾ cup red wine

1½ tbsp concentrated beef stock or 1 beef bouillon cube

salt and pepper

Lasagna

1. Heat the oil in a pan. Add the ground beef, onion, garlic, and carrot and cook over medium heat, stirring frequently and breaking up the meat with a wooden spoon, for 5–8 minutes, until the beef is evenly browned.

2. Stir in the herbs, season to taste with salt and pepper, and pour in the strained pureed tomatoes. Bring to a boil, then reduce the heat, cover, and simmer for 15 minutes.

3. Meanwhile, preheat the oven to 375°F/190°C. Combine the ricotta and beaten egg, stirring until smooth.

4. Make alternating layers of the ground beef mixture, lasagna noodles, the ricotta mixture, and mozzarella in an ovenproof dish, ending with a layer of mozzarella. Bake in the preheated oven for 40–45 minutes, until the topping is golden and bubbling. Remove from the oven and let stand for 5 minutes before serving.

Serves 6

2 tbsp olive oil

1 lb 2 oz/500 g ground beef

1 onion, chopped

1 garlic clove, finely chopped

1 carrot, diced

1 tbsp chopped fresh flat-leaf parsley

6 basil leaves, torn

2½ cups strained pureed tomatoes

2½ cups ricotta cheese

1 egg, lightly beaten

8 lasagna noodles, cooked according to package directions

2 cups grated mozzarella cheese

salt and pepper

Beefy Baked Potatoes

1. Preheat the oven to 425°F/220°C. Prick the potatoes all over with a fork to let steam escape during baking. Put them directly on an oven shelf and bake in the preheated oven for 1¼–1½ hours, until soft.

2. Meanwhile, heat the oil in a pan. Add the chopped scallions and the garlic and cook over low heat, stirring occasionally, for 5 minutes, until softened. Add the ground beef, increase the heat to medium, and cook, stirring frequently and breaking it up with a wooden spoon, for 8–10 minutes, until evenly browned.

3. Stir in the tomato paste, soy sauce, and ⅔ cup of the stock and season to taste with salt and pepper. Reduce the heat, cover, and simmer, stirring occasionally, for 25–30 minutes, adding more stock if the mixture seems to be drying out.

4. Remove the potatoes from the oven and put them on 4 individual plates. Cut a cross in the center of each and squeeze gently, then ladle the ground beef mixture over them. Garnish with shredded scallions and serve immediately.

Serves 4

4 large baking potatoes
2 tbsp sunflower oil
2 scallions, finely chopped, plus extra shredded scallions to garnish
1 garlic clove, finely chopped
12 oz/350 g ground beef
1 tbsp tomato paste
1 tbsp light soy sauce
⅔–1 cup beef stock
salt and pepper

Battered Beef

1. First, make the batter. Sift the flour, cayenne pepper, and salt into a bowl. Make a well in the center and add the egg and half the milk. Stir together with a wooden spoon, gradually incorporating the dry ingredients, then beat well with a whisk or electric mixer until smooth and full of bubbles. Stir in the remaining milk, cover the bowl, and let rest for 30 minutes.

2. Meanwhile, preheat the oven to 400°F/200°C. Combine the ground beef, onion, garlic, and parsley in a bowl and season to taste with salt and pepper.

3. Heat the oil in a shallow baking pan until very hot, then remove from the heat. Stir the batter and pour half of it into the pan. Spread the ground beef mixture on top, using a spatula, and pour the remaining batter over it.

4. Bake in the preheated oven for 20 minutes, until the batter is bubbling, then reduce the oven temperature to 350°F/180°C and bake for an additional 30 minutes, until golden brown.

5. Garnish with parsley and cut into squares. Serve immediately.

Serves 6

- 1 lb 7 oz/650 g ground beef
- ½ onion, finely chopped
- 1 garlic clove, finely chopped
- 1 tbsp finely chopped fresh parsley, plus extra to garnish
- 2 tbsp sunflower oil
- salt and pepper

Batter
1 cup all-purpose flour
pinch of cayenne pepper
pinch of salt
1 extra large egg
1¼ cups milk

Savory Croquettes

1. Heat the oil in a skillet. Add the onion and garlic and cook over low–medium heat, stirring occasionally, for 8–10 minutes, until golden brown.

2. Transfer the onion and garlic to a large bowl, add the ground beef, 1 of the eggs, the sour cream, chopped parsley, paprika, and ½ cup of the breadcrumbs, and season to taste with salt and pepper. Using your hands, mix well until all the ingredients are thoroughly combined. Shape the mixture into 12 equal-size croquettes.

3. Lightly beat the remaining eggs in a shallow dish and spread out the remaining breadcrumbs in a separate shallow dish. Coat the croquettes first in beaten egg and then in breadcrumbs.

4. Melt the butter in a large skillet. Add the croquettes, in batches if necessary, and cook over medium heat for 5–6 minutes on each side, until evenly browned and cooked through. Remove from the skillet with a spatula and keep warm while you cook the remaining batches. Garnish with parsley sprigs and serve immediately.

Serves 6

2 tbsp sunflower oil

1 Bermuda onion, finely chopped

2 garlic cloves, finely chopped

2 lb 4 oz/1 kg ground beef

3 eggs

2 tbsp sour cream

1 tbsp chopped fresh flat-leaf parsley, plus extra sprigs to garnish

1 tsp sweet paprika

2 cups fresh breadcrumbs

6 tbsp butter

salt and pepper

Beef & Potato Rissoles

1. Cook the potatoes in a large pan of salted boiling water for 25–30 minutes, until tender but not falling apart. Drain well, turn into a bowl, and mash until smooth.

2. Add the onion, ground beef, chives, parsley, and Worcestershire sauce, then season to taste with salt and pepper. Mix well until thoroughly combined. If you have time, cover the bowl with plastic wrap and chill in the refrigerator for 30–45 minutes to firm up.

3. Damp your hands and shape the mixture into 12 sausage shapes. Lightly beat the eggs in a shallow dish, spread out the flour in a separate shallow dish, and spread out the breadcrumbs in a third shallow dish.

4. Pour oil into a large skillet to a depth of about ½ inch/1 cm and heat. Meanwhile, coat the rissoles first in the flour, then in the beaten egg, and, finally, in the breadcrumbs. Shake off any excess.

5. Add the rissoles to the skillet, in batches if necessary, and cook over medium heat, turning occasionally, for 8–10 minutes, until crispy, evenly browned, and cooked through. Remove from the skillet with a slotted spatula and keep warm while you cook the remaining rissoles. Serve immediately.

Serves 6

2 lb 4 oz/1 kg potatoes
1 onion, finely chopped
1 lb 2 oz/500 g ground beef
1 tbsp snipped fresh chives
1 tbsp chopped fresh parsley
2 tsp Worcestershire sauce or ketchup
3 eggs
3 tbsp all-purpose flour
3 cups fresh breadcrumbs
sunflower oil, for shallow-frying
salt and pepper

Cabbage Rolls

1. Preheat the oven to 375°F/190°C. Brush an ovenproof dish with oil.

2. Bring a large pan of water to a boil. Add the cabbage leaves, bring back to a boil, and blanch for 1 minute. Remove with tongs and drain on paper towels.

3. Put the scallions, garlic, ground beef, and sage into a bowl, season to taste with salt and pepper, and mix well until thoroughly combined.

4. Divide the ground beef mixture into 12 equal-size portions and shape each into a sausage shape. Place 1 piece on the stalk end of a cabbage leaf and roll up, tucking in the sides. Put the roll, seam-side down, into the prepared dish. Repeat with the remaining ground beef mixture and cabbage leaves, arranging them in a single layer in the dish.

5. Sprinkle the sugar evenly over the cabbage rolls and pour the tomatoes, with the can juices, over the top. Cover with aluminum foil and bake in the preheated oven for 1 hour, until tender. Serve immediately.

Serves 4–6

olive oil, for brushing

12 large green cabbage or Swiss chard leaves, coarse stalks removed

4 scallions, finely chopped

1 garlic clove, finely chopped

12 oz/350 g ground beef

1 fresh sage sprig, finely chopped

2 tbsp dark brown sugar

14 oz/400 g canned chopped tomatoes

salt and pepper

Stuffed Onions

1. Cut a thin slice from the bottom of the onions and make a circular cut around the top of each. Add the onions to a pan of salted boiling water, cover, and simmer for 20 minutes. Meanwhile, place the bread in a heatproof bowl with the milk and let soak.

2. Remove the onions from the pan using a slotted spoon. Stir the concentrated stock into the cooking liquid and set aside. When the onions are cool enough to handle, scoop out the flesh from the centers without piercing the shells.

3. Preheat the oven to 350°F/180°C. Squeeze out the bread and put it into a bowl with the ground beef, garlic, cumin, coriander, 1 tablespoon of the cooking liquid, and about three-quarters of the beaten egg. Season to taste with salt and pepper and mix well. Using a teaspoon, fill the scooped-out onions with the mixture. Brush the tops with the remaining beaten egg and dust the onions all over with flour.

4. Heat enough oil for deep-frying in a deep-fryer to 350–375°F/180–190°C, or until a cube of bread browns in 30 seconds. Add the stuffed onions, in batches if necessary, and cook for 5–8 minutes, until evenly browned. Heat the 2 tablespoons of oil in a casserole. Put the onions into the casserole in a single layer and ladle in enough of the cooking liquid to come about halfway up them. Cover and bake in the preheated oven for 30 minutes, until tender. Serve immediately.

Serves 6

12 small onions, peeled

2 slices white bread, crusts removed, halved

¾ cup hot milk

2 tbsp concentrated beef stock or 1 beef bouillon cube

10 oz/280 g ground beef

1 small garlic clove, finely chopped

½ tsp ground cumin

½ tsp ground coriander

2 eggs, lightly beaten

all-purpose flour, for dusting

2 tbsp sunflower oil, plus extra for deep-frying

salt and pepper

Meaty Muffins

1. Preheat the oven to 400°F/200°C. Generously grease a 12-cup muffin pan.

2. Put the ground beef, onion, corn, and parsley into a bowl, season to taste with salt and pepper, and mix well until thoroughly combined.

3. Sift the flour, baking powder, and a pinch of salt into a separate bowl and make a well in the center. Lightly beat the eggs with the milk and oil in a third bowl, then pour into the well and gradually incorporate the dry ingredients until thoroughly combined.

4. Spoon a little of the batter into each cup in the muffin pan so that each muffin cup is a quarter full. Divide the ground beef mixture among the muffin cups and sprinkle with half the cheese. Top with the remaining batter and sprinkle with the remaining cheese. Bake in the preheated oven for 20 minutes, until golden and the muffins spring back when lightly pressed. Serve hot or warm.

Makes 12

butter, for greasing
12 oz/350 g ground beef
1 small onion, very finely chopped
5 oz/140 g canned corn kernels, drained
1 tbsp chopped fresh parsley
2¼ cups all-purpose flour
2 tsp baking powder
2 eggs
generous 1 cup milk
½ cup sunflower oil
1 cup grated cheddar cheese
salt and pepper

Favorite

22

Meatballs

1. Tear the bread into pieces and put it into a bowl. Pour in water to cover and let soak for 5 minutes.

2. Put the ground beef, onion, ketchup, and egg into a bowl and season to taste with salt and pepper. Squeeze out the bread, add it to the bowl, and mix well with your hands until thoroughly combined and smooth. Add the 3 tablespoons of water and knead for 5 minutes. Set aside while you make the sauce.

3. For the tomato sauce, heat the oil in a pan. Add the onion and garlic and cook over low heat, stirring occasionally, for 5 minutes, until softened. Meanwhile, mix the tomato paste with the scant ½ cup of water in a small bowl. Add the tomato paste mixture and the tomatoes to the pan and bring to a boil, then simmer, stirring occasionally, for 15–20 minutes, until thickened. Transfer the sauce to a food processor or blender and process until smooth. Pour into a clean pan, stir in sugar to taste, and season to taste with salt and pepper.

4. Meanwhile, shape the ground beef mixture into 20 small balls, rolling them between the palms of your hands.

5. Bring the sauce back to a simmer, then add the meatballs and simmer gently, occasionally shaking the pan, for 30 minutes, until cooked through. Garnish with parsley and serve immediately.

Serves 4

3 slices white bread, crusts removed

1 lb 7 oz/650 g ground beef

1 onion, grated

½ cup ketchup

1 egg, lightly beaten

3 tbsp water

salt and pepper

chopped fresh parsley, to garnish

Tomato sauce

2 tbsp sunflower oil

1 onion, finely chopped

2 garlic cloves, finely chopped

2 tbsp tomato paste

scant ½ cup water

14 oz/400 g canned chopped tomatoes

1–2 tsp brown sugar

salt and pepper

23

Swedish Meatballs

1. Cook the potatoes in a pan of salted boiling water for 20–25 minutes, until tender but not falling apart. Drain, put into a bowl, mash well, and let cool slightly.

2. Add the fresh breadcrumbs, ground beef, onion, egg, sugar, and spices to the bowl. Season to taste with salt and pepper and mix well until thoroughly combined. Shape the mixture into walnut-size balls, rolling them between the palms of your hands. Roll the meatballs in the dry breadcrumbs until thoroughly coated.

3. Melt the butter in a large skillet. Add the meatballs, in batches, and cook over medium heat, stirring and turning occasionally, for 10 minutes, until golden brown all over and cooked through. Remove with a slotted spoon, drain on paper towels, and keep warm while you cook the remaining batches.

4. When all the meatballs have been cooked, keep them warm while you make the sauce. Stir the flour into the skillet and cook, stirring constantly, for 1 minute. Remove the skillet from the heat and gradually stir in the stock, then add the cream. Season to taste with salt and pepper, return the skillet to low heat, and cook, stirring constantly, until thickened and smooth.

5. Return the meatballs to the skillet and simmer for 10 minutes. Serve immediately.

Serves 4

2 potatoes, cut into chunks
½ cup fresh breadcrumbs
1 lb 7 oz/650 g ground beef
1 small onion, grated
1 egg, lightly beaten
1 tsp brown sugar
pinch each of grated nutmeg, ground allspice, ground ginger, and ground cloves
¾ cup fine dry breadcrumbs
6 tbsp butter
salt and pepper

Sauce
2 tbsp all-purpose flour
1 cup beef stock
1 cup heavy cream
salt and pepper

Meat Loaf

1. Preheat the oven to 325°F/160°C. Put the ground beef, onion, garlic (if using), mushrooms, breadcrumbs, eggs, mustard, Worcestershire sauce, celery salt, and parsley into a bowl, season to taste with pepper, and mix well until thoroughly combined.

2. Spoon the mixture into a 9 x 5 x 3-inch/23 x 13 x 8-cm loaf pan, pressing it down well. Cover with the bacon.

3. Put the loaf pan into a roasting pan and pour in boiling water to come about halfway up the sides. Bake in the preheated oven for 1½ hours, until a wooden toothpick inserted into the center comes out clean.

4. Remove the pan from the oven and pour off any fat. Let cool for 1 hour. Run a round-bladed knife around the sides of the pan and turn out the meat loaf onto a plate. Wrap the loaf in aluminum foil and chill in the refrigerator for 4 hours, or overnight. Cut into slices and serve with the tomato sauce.

Serves 4

* 1 lb 2 oz/500 g ground beef
* 1 onion, finely chopped
* 2 garlic cloves, finely chopped (optional)
* 1⅔ cups finely chopped mushrooms
* 1½ cups fresh breadcrumbs
* 2 eggs, lightly beaten
* 2 tsp Dijon mustard
* 1 tsp Worcestershire sauce
* 1 tsp celery salt
* 1 tbsp chopped fresh parsley
* 8–10 bacon slices
* pepper
* 1 quantity Tomato Sauce, to serve (see page 58)

Spaghetti Bolognese

1. Heat the oil in a pan. Add the bacon, onion, carrot, celery, and garlic and cook over low heat, stirring occasionally, for 5 minutes, until softened.

2. Add the ground beef, increase the heat to medium, and cook, stirring frequently and breaking up the meat with a wooden spoon, for 8–10 minutes, until evenly browned. Stir in the mushrooms and chicken livers, if using, and cook, stirring frequently, for an additional 3–4 minutes.

3. Stir in the tomatoes, tomato paste, wine, stock, bay leaf, and oregano, season to taste with salt and pepper, and bring to a boil. Reduce the heat, cover, and simmer, stirring occasionally, for 1 hour.

4. Shortly before the sauce is ready, bring a pan of salted water to a boil. Add the spaghetti, bring back to a boil, and cook for 8–10 minutes, until tender but still firm to the bite. Drain the pasta, return it to the pan, and toss with the butter.

5. Remove the sauce from the heat and discard the bay leaf. Add the spaghetti and toss well, then transfer to a warmed serving dish. Sprinkle with Parmesan cheese shavings and serve immediately.

Serves 4

2 tbsp olive oil

3 slices bacon, chopped

1 onion, finely chopped

1 carrot, finely chopped

1 celery stalk, finely chopped

2 garlic cloves, finely chopped

1 lb 2 oz/500 g ground beef

1⅔ cups thinly sliced mushrooms

4 oz/115 g chicken livers, finely chopped (optional)

14 oz/400 g canned chopped tomatoes

2 tbsp tomato paste

⅔ cup white wine

1¼ cups beef stock

1 bay leaf

pinch of dried oregano

1 lb/450 g dried spaghetti

2 tbsp butter

salt and pepper

Parmesan cheese shavings, to serve

26

Meaty Macaroni & Cheese

1. Heat the oil in a pan. Add the onion and garlic and cook over low heat, stirring occasionally, for 5 minutes, until softened. Add the ground beef, increase the heat to medium, and cook, breaking it up with a wooden spoon, for 8–10 minutes, until lightly browned all over. Stir in the corn, tomatoes, and mixed herbs and season to taste with salt and pepper. Reduce the heat, cover, and simmer, stirring occasionally, for 25–30 minutes.

2. Bring a large pan of salted water to a boil. Add the macaroni, bring back to a boil, and cook for 10 minutes, until tender but still firm to the bite.

3. Meanwhile, melt the butter in a separate pan. Sprinkle in the flour and cook, stirring constantly, for 2 minutes. Remove the pan from the heat and gradually stir in the milk, a little at a time. Return the pan to the heat and bring to a boil, stirring constantly. Reduce the heat and simmer the sauce, stirring constantly, for 5 minutes, until thickened and smooth. Remove the pan from the heat and stir in the mustard and 1⅓ cups of the cheese. Stir well until the cheese has melted.

4. Preheat the broiler. Drain the macaroni and put it into the cheese sauce, stirring well to mix. Spoon the ground beef mixture into a flameproof dish, then cover with the macaroni mixture. Sprinkle with the remaining cheese and cook under the preheated broiler for a few minutes, until golden and bubbling. Serve immediately.

Serves 6

2 tbsp olive oil

1 onion, chopped

1 garlic clove, finely chopped

1 lb 2 oz/500 g ground beef

7 oz/200g canned corn kernels, drained

14 oz/400 g canned chopped tomatoes

1 tsp dried mixed herbs

8 oz/225 g dried macaroni

3 tbsp butter

⅓ cup all-purpose flour

2¼ cups milk

2 tsp Dijon mustard

1¾ cups grated cheddar cheese

salt and pepper

Spaghetti & Meatballs

1. Heat the oil in a skillet. Add the chopped onion and garlic and cook over low heat for 5 minutes, until softened. Remove from the heat and put the mixture into a bowl with the thyme, ground beef, breadcrumbs, and egg. Season to taste with salt and pepper, then mix well. Shape into 20 meatballs.

2. Heat a large nonstick skillet over low–medium heat. Add the meatballs and cook, stirring gently and turning frequently, for 15 minutes, until lightly browned all over.

3. Meanwhile, preheat the broiler. To make the sauce, put the onion wedges and bell pepper halves, skin-side up, on a broiler rack and cook under the preheated broiler, turning frequently, for 10 minutes, until the bell pepper skins are blistered and charred. Put the bell peppers into a plastic bag, tie the top, and let cool. Set the onion wedges aside.

4. Peel off the bell pepper skins. Coarsely chop the flesh and put it into a food processor or blender with the onion wedges and tomatoes. Process to a smooth paste and season to taste with salt and pepper. Pour into a pan, add the bay leaf, and bring to a boil. Reduce the heat and simmer, stirring occasionally, for 10 minutes. Remove and discard the bay leaf.

5. Meanwhile, bring a large pan of salted water to a boil. Add the spaghetti, bring back to a boil, and cook for 10 minutes, until tender but still firm to the bite. Drain the spaghetti and serve immediately with the meatballs and sauce.

Serves 4

1 tbsp olive oil

1 small onion, finely chopped

2 garlic cloves, finely chopped

2 fresh thyme sprigs, finely chopped

1 lb 7 oz/650 g ground beef

½ cup fresh breadcrumbs

1 egg, lightly beaten

1 lb/450 g dried spaghetti

salt and pepper

Sauce

1 onion, cut into wedges

3 red bell peppers, halved and seeded

14 oz/400 g canned chopped tomatoes

1 bay leaf

salt and pepper

Béchamel Lasagna

① Heat the oil in a pan. Add the bacon and cook, stirring frequently, for 3–4 minutes. Add the onion, garlic, carrots, and celery and cook over low heat, stirring occasionally, for 5 minutes, until softened. Add the ground beef, increase the heat to medium, and cook, stirring frequently and breaking it up with a wooden spoon, for 8–10 minutes, until evenly browned. Stir in the oregano, parsley, and tomatoes. Season to taste with salt and pepper, reduce the heat, and simmer, stirring occasionally, for 30 minutes.

② Meanwhile, preheat the oven to 400°F/200°C. To make the béchamel sauce, pour the milk into a pan and add the peppercorns, onion, bay leaf, and mace. Bring just to a boil, then remove the pan from the heat and let steep for 10 minutes. Strain the milk into a pitcher and discard the flavorings. Melt the butter in a separate pan. Stir in the flour and cook, stirring constantly, for 2 minutes. Gradually stir in the flavored milk, a little at a time, and bring to a boil, stirring constantly. Reduce the heat and simmer, stirring constantly, for a few minutes, until thickened and smooth. Remove the pan from the heat and season to taste with salt and pepper.

③ Make alternating layers of the ground beef mixture, lasagna noodles, béchamel sauce, and Parmesan in an ovenproof dish, ending with a layer of béchamel sauce sprinkled with Parmesan. Bake in the preheated oven for 30 minutes, until golden brown. Let stand for 10 minutes before serving.

Serves 6

3 tbsp olive oil

2 bacon slices

1 Bermuda onion, chopped

2 garlic cloves, finely chopped

2 carrots, chopped

2 celery stalks, chopped

12 oz/350 g ground beef

pinch of dried oregano

1 tbsp chopped fresh parsley

14 oz/400 g canned chopped tomatoes

8 oz/225 g lasagna noodles, cooked according to package directions

1⅓ cups grated Parmesan cheese

salt and pepper

Béchamel sauce

2¼ cups milk

6 black peppercorns

1 slice onion

1 bay leaf

1 mace blade

4 tbsp butter

½ cup all-purpose flour

salt and pepper

29

Sloppy Joes

1. Put the ground beef, onion, garlic, and bell pepper into a nonstick skillet and cook, stirring frequently and breaking up the beef with a wooden spoon, over medium heat for 8–10 minutes, until the beef is evenly browned. Carefully drain off the fat.

2. Stir in the mustard, ketchup, vinegar, sugar, and spice, if using. Season to taste with salt and pepper. Reduce the heat and simmer, stirring occasionally, for 30 minutes.

3. Divide the mixture among the hamburger buns and serve immediately.

Serves 4

1 lb/450 g ground beef

1 onion, chopped

1 garlic clove, chopped

1 green bell pepper, seeded and chopped

1 tbsp mild mustard

¾ cup ketchup

1 tsp white vinegar

1 tbsp brown sugar

pinch of chili powder, ground cloves, or paprika (optional)

4 hamburger buns, split

salt and pepper

Cheese-Stuffed Hamburgers

1. Preheat the broiler. Put the ground beef, onion, garlic, horseradish, and thyme into a bowl. Season to taste with salt and pepper and mix well until thoroughly combined. Divide the mixture into 8 portions and shape each into a patty.

2. Sprinkle the cheese over 4 of the patties and top with the remaining patties. Gently press the edges together, smoothing them with a spatula to enclose the cheese completely.

3. Cook under the preheated broiler for 5–6 minutes on each side, turning them carefully with a spatula. Serve in the toasted hamburger buns with arugula leaves.

Serves 4

* 1 lb 2 oz/500 g ground beef
* 1 onion, finely chopped
* 1 garlic clove, finely chopped
  1 tsp creamed horseradish
  1 tbsp chopped fresh thyme
  ½ cup crumbled Gorgonzola or feta cheese
  4 hamburger buns, split and toasted
* salt and pepper
  arugula leaves, to serve

Stuffed Bell Peppers

1. Cut off the tops of the bell peppers and remove the seeds and membranes without piercing the shells, then set aside. Cut out the stems from the sliced tops and chop the flesh.

2. Heat the oil in a skillet. Add the onions, garlic, chiles, and chopped bell pepper and cook over low heat, stirring occasionally, for 5 minutes, until softened. Add the ground beef and Tabasco and season to taste with salt. Increase the heat to medium and cook, stirring frequently and breaking up the beef with a wooden spoon, for 8–10 minutes, until evenly browned. Stir in the flour, then gradually stir in the stock. Bring to a boil, stirring constantly, then reduce the heat, cover, and simmer for 30 minutes.

3. Meanwhile, preheat the oven to 350°F/180°C. Brush an ovenproof dish with oil. Remove the skillet from the heat and spoon the ground beef mixture into the bell peppers. Stand them upright in the prepared dish and bake in the preheated oven for 45 minutes.

4. Put the cream, cream cheese, and cayenne pepper into a pan, season to taste with salt, and stir until smooth. Add the golden raisins and cook over medium heat, stirring constantly, until hot. Do not let the mixture boil.

5. Remove the bell peppers from the oven and pour the cream cheese sauce over them. Return to the oven and bake for an additional 15 minutes. Serve immediately.

Serves 4

4 large red bell peppers
3 tbsp sunflower oil, plus extra
 for brushing
2 onions, finely chopped
2 garlic cloves, finely chopped
2 fresh green chiles, seeded
 and finely chopped
1 lb 2 oz/500 g ground beef
1 tsp Tabasco sauce
2 tbsp all-purpose flour
1 cup beef stock
⅔ cup light cream
1 cup cream cheese
pinch of cayenne pepper
¾ cup golden raisins
salt

32

Ground Beef & Mashed Vegetables

1. Heat the oil in a skillet. Add the onion and carrots and cook over low heat, stirring occasionally, for 5 minutes, until softened. Add the ground beef, increase the heat to medium, and cook, stirring frequently and breaking it up with a wooden spoon, for 8–10 minutes, until evenly browned.

2. Stir in the thyme and oats and pour in the stock. Season to taste with salt and pepper, then bring to a boil. Reduce the heat, cover, and simmer, stirring occasionally, for 25–30 minutes, until thickened.

3. Meanwhile, cook the parsnips and potatoes in a large pan of salted boiling water for 10–15 minutes, until tender but not falling apart, then remove from the heat and drain. Return the vegetables to the pan, add the butter and cream, and season to taste with salt and pepper. Mash well until smooth.

4. Divide the mashed vegetables among individual plates. Top with the ground beef mixture, garnish with parsley sprigs, and serve immediately.

Serves 6

2 tbsp sunflower oil

1 onion, finely chopped

2 carrots, finely chopped

2 lb 4 oz/1 kg ground beef

1 tbsp chopped fresh thyme

2 tbsp rolled oats

1 cup beef stock

2 lb 4 oz/1 kg parsnips, finely chopped

2 lb 4 oz/1 kg potatoes, finely chopped

½ cup butter

6 tbsp heavy cream

salt and pepper

fresh flat-leaf parsley sprigs, to garnish

Stuffed Baked Potatoes

1. Preheat the oven to 425°F/220°C. Prick the potatoes all over with a fork to let steam escape during baking. Put them directly on an oven shelf and bake in the preheated oven for 1¼–1½ hours, until soft.

2. Meanwhile, heat the oil in a large pan. Add the bacon and cook over low heat, stirring occasionally, for 5 minutes. Add the onion, garlic, and celery and cook, stirring occasionally, for 5 minutes, until softened. Add the ground beef, increase the heat to medium, and cook, stirring frequently and breaking it up with a wooden spoon, for 8–10 minutes, until evenly browned. Add the tomatoes, ketchup, Worcestershire sauce, sage, and thyme and season to taste with salt and pepper. Reduce the heat, cover, and simmer, stirring occasionally, for 30 minutes.

3. Remove the potatoes from the oven and reduce the oven temperature to 375°F/190°C. Cut off a slice from each potato and carefully scoop out the flesh into a bowl. Spoon the ground beef mixture into the potato shells to fill them halfway. Mash the scooped-out potato with the butter and cheese and spoon it into the shells on top of the ground beef mixture. Put the potatoes into an ovenproof dish, fluff up the potato topping with a fork, and bake for an additional 15–20 minutes. Serve immediately.

Serves 4

4 large baking potatoes
2 tbsp sunflower oil
4 bacon slices, finely chopped
1 onion, finely chopped
1 garlic clove, finely chopped
1 celery stalk, finely chopped
1 lb/450 g ground beef
14 oz/400 g canned chopped tomatoes
1 tbsp ketchup
1 tbsp Worcestershire sauce
1 tsp chopped fresh sage
1 tsp chopped fresh thyme
6 tbsp butter
¾ cup crumbled feta cheese
salt and pepper

Ground Beef Pizza

1. Preheat the oven to 400°F/200°C. Brush a baking sheet with oil. To make the pizza dough, sift the flour and salt into a bowl. Add the butter, cut it into the dry ingredients, and rub in with your fingertips until the mixture resembles breadcrumbs. Pour in most of the milk and mix with a round-bladed knife to form a soft dough, adding the remaining milk if needed. Turn out the dough onto a lightly floured surface and knead gently. Roll out to a 10-inch/25-cm circle and transfer to the prepared baking sheet. Push up the edge slightly all around to make a rim.

2. Put the ground beef, onion, garlic, and cumin in a nonstick skillet and cook over medium heat, stirring frequently and breaking up the meat with a wooden spoon, for 5–8 minutes, until evenly browned. Stir in the bell pepper and cilantro and season to taste with salt and pepper.

3. Spread the tomato paste over the pizza crust and cover with the ground beef mixture. Top with the mozzarella and drizzle with oil. Bake in the preheated oven for 15–20 minutes, until the crust is crispy. Serve immediately.

Serves 2

olive oil, for brushing and drizzling

6 oz/175 g ground beef

1 small onion, finely chopped

1 garlic clove, finely chopped

1 tsp ground cumin

½–1 charbroiled red bell pepper in oil, drained and finely chopped

1 tbsp chopped fresh cilantro

4 tbsp tomato paste

4 oz/115 g mozzarella cheese, sliced

salt and pepper

Pizza dough

1½ cups self-rising flour, plus extra for dusting

pinch of salt

2 tbsp butter

½ cup milk

35

Beef in Pita Pockets

1. Heat the oil in a skillet. Add the onion and garlic and cook over low heat, stirring occasionally, for 5 minutes, until softened. Add the ground beef, increase the heat to medium, and cook, stirring frequently and breaking it up with a wooden spoon, for 8–10 minutes, until evenly browned. Stir in the tomatoes and spices, then season to taste with salt and pepper. Reduce the heat and simmer, stirring occasionally, for 15–20 minutes.

2. Meanwhile, dry-fry the pine nuts in a small skillet, stirring constantly, for a few minutes, until golden, then remove the skillet from the heat. Stir the pine nuts and cilantro into the ground beef mixture and simmer for an additional few minutes.

3. To serve, cut a slit in the side of each pita bread to make a pocket. Put a little of the ground beef mixture, some chopped cucumber, and shredded lettuce into each pocket and top with a spoonful of sour cream.

Serves 4

2 tbsp olive oil
1 onion, chopped
1 garlic clove, chopped
1 lb 2 oz/500 g ground beef
7 oz/200 g canned chopped tomatoes
1 tsp ground cumin
1 tsp ground coriander
½ tsp ground turmeric
¾ cup pine nuts
2 tbsp chopped fresh cilantro
salt and pepper

To serve
8 pita breads, warmed
chopped cucumber
shredded lettuce
sour cream

36

Beef 'n' Beans

1. Put the onion and ground beef into a large nonstick skillet and cook over medium heat, stirring frequently and breaking up the meat with a wooden spoon, for 8–10 minutes, until evenly browned.

2. Stir the baked beans, maple syrup, mustard, and concentrated stock into the skillet and season to taste with pepper. Reduce the heat, cover, and simmer, stirring occasionally, for 15 minutes, adding a little water if the mixture seems to be drying out.

3. Meanwhile, cook the potatoes in a pan of salted boiling water for 20 minutes, until tender but not falling apart. Drain the potatoes, return to the pan, and add the cream cheese. Season to taste with salt and pepper and mash until smooth.

4. Preheat the broiler. Transfer the ground beef mixture to a flameproof dish and spread the mashed potatoes over the top. Cook under the preheated broiler for 5 minutes, until the topping is golden brown. Serve immediately.

Serves 4

- 1 onion, chopped
- 1 lb 2 oz/500 g ground beef
- 14 oz/400 g canned baked beans
- 1 tbsp maple syrup
- 1 tbsp mild mustard
- 1 tbsp concentrated beef stock
- 1 lb 7 oz/650 g potatoes, diced
- ½ cup cream cheese
- salt and pepper

Ground Beef Hash

1. Cook the potatoes in a pan of salted boiling water for 20–25 minutes, until tender but not falling apart. Drain and let cool.

2. Meanwhile, combine the ground beef, bell pepper, paprika, and parsley in a bowl and season to taste with salt and pepper. Dice the potatoes and add them to the mixture, stirring gently until thoroughly combined.

3. Heat the oil in a large skillet. Add the onion and cook over low heat, stirring occasionally, for 5 minutes, until softened.

4. Add the ground beef mixture to the skillet and shake the skillet to mix it with the onion, then press down gently with a wooden spoon. Cook over medium heat, without stirring, for 5 minutes, until browned on the underside. Stir well, then cook, without stirring, for 5 minutes. Repeat the stirring and cooking twice more until the mixture is evenly browned.

5. Reduce the heat to low. Make 2 hollows in the mixture with the back of a spoon. Crack an egg into each hollow, cover, and cook for an additional 5 minutes, until the whites have set. Cut the hash into halves, each with an egg, garnish with parsley, and serve immediately.

Serves 2

3 potatoes, cut into chunks

12 oz/350 g ground beef

1 red bell pepper, seeded and finely chopped

½ tsp sweet paprika

1 tbsp chopped fresh parsley, plus extra to garnish

3 tbsp sunflower oil

1 onion, finely chopped

2 eggs

salt and pepper

38

Simple Savory Beef

1. Melt the butter in a pan. Add the onion and carrots and cook over low heat, stirring occasionally, for 5 minutes, until softened. Add the tomatoes and cook, stirring occasionally, for an additional 3 minutes.

2. Remove the pan from the heat and stir in the flour and dry mustard, then return to the heat and cook, stirring constantly, for 2 minutes. Gradually stir in the stock, a little at a time, then bring to a boil, stirring constantly. Cook, stirring constantly, for an additional few minutes, until thickened.

3. Add the ground beef and stir to break it up. Season to taste with salt and pepper, cover, and simmer, stirring occasionally, for 45 minutes.

4. Gently stir in the peas, re-cover the pan, and simmer, stirring occasionally, for an additional 15 minutes. Taste and adjust the seasoning, adding salt and pepper if needed. Garnish with parsley and serve immediately.

Serves 4

4 tbsp butter

1 Bermuda onion, finely chopped

2 carrots, finely chopped

4 tomatoes, peeled and chopped

¼ cup all-purpose flour

1 tsp dry mustard

2½ cups beef stock

1 lb 2 oz/500 g ground beef

1½ cups frozen peas

salt and pepper

chopped fresh parsley, to garnish

39

Salisbury Steak

1. Put the onion, breadcrumbs, and egg into a bowl and mix well. Combine the undiluted soup, horseradish, Worcestershire sauce, and mustard in a separate bowl, stirring until thoroughly combined.

2. Add 4 tablespoons of the soup mixture to the onion mixture, then stir in the ground beef and season to taste with salt and pepper. Mix well until thoroughly combined. Divide the mixture into 6 portions and shape them into patties.

3. Heat the oil in a large skillet. Add the patties and cook over medium heat for 3–4 minutes on each side, until lightly browned.

4. Stir the stock into the remaining soup mixture and pour it into the skillet. Reduce the heat, cover, and simmer for 12–15 minutes, until the patties are cooked through. Garnish with parsley and serve immediately.

Serves 6

1 small onion, finely chopped

generous ⅓ cup dry breadcrumbs

1 egg, lightly beaten

1¼ cups canned condensed cream of mushroom soup

1 tsp creamed horseradish

1 tbsp Worcestershire sauce

1 tbsp Dijon mustard

1 lb 9 oz/700 g ground beef

2 tbsp sunflower oil

½ cup beef stock

salt and pepper

chopped fresh parsley, to garnish

Comforting

40

Tamale Pie

1. Preheat the oven to 375°F/190°C. Heat the oil in a large skillet. Add the onion and cook over low heat, stirring occasionally, for 5 minutes, until softened.

2. Add the ground beef, increase the heat to medium, and cook, stirring frequently and breaking it up with the spoon, for 8–10 minutes, until evenly browned. Stir in the chili powder, tomatoes, corn, olives, and sour cream and season to taste with salt, then transfer the mixture to an ovenproof dish.

3. Put the cornmeal, baking powder, butter, and milk in a food processor and process until combined. With the motor running, gradually add enough of the stock through the feeder tube to make a thick, smooth mixture.

4. Pour the cornmeal mixture over the ground beef mixture and smooth the surface with a spatula. Bake in the preheated oven for 20 minutes, until the topping is just beginning to brown. Sprinkle with the cheese, return to the oven, and bake for an additional 15 minutes, until golden and bubbling. Serve immediately.

Serves 6

2 tbsp corn oil

✳ 1 onion, finely chopped

✳ 12 oz/350 g ground beef

1½ tsp chili powder

7 oz/200 g canned chopped tomatoes

5 oz/140 g canned corn kernels, drained

2 tbsp chopped pitted black olives

scant ½ cup sour cream

generous 1 cup cornmeal

½ tsp baking powder

4 tbsp butter, cut into pieces

3 tbsp milk

about 1 cup hot chicken stock

¾ cup grated cheddar cheese

✳ salt

41

Ground Beef with Potato Topping

1. Cook the potatoes in a large pan of salted boiling water for 20–25 minutes, until tender but not falling apart.

2. Meanwhile, heat the oil in a pan. Add the onion, garlic (if using), and carrots and cook over low heat, stirring occasionally, for 5 minutes, until the onion has softened. Increase the heat to medium, add the ground beef, and cook, stirring frequently and breaking it up with a wooden spoon, for 8–10 minutes, until evenly browned.

3. Add the mushrooms and cook for 2 minutes, then pour in the stock and stir in the sugar and Worcestershire sauce. Season to taste with salt and pepper. Reduce the heat, cover, and simmer for 20 minutes.

4. Preheat the oven to 400°F/200°C. Drain the potatoes, return to the pan, and mash well, then stir in three-quarters of the cheese.

5. Spoon the meat mixture into an ovenproof dish and spread the mashed potatoes over the top to cover. Sprinkle with the remaining cheese and bake in the preheated oven for 20 minutes, until the topping is golden brown. Serve immediately.

Serves 6

1 lb 7 oz/650 g potatoes, cut into chunks

2 tbsp sunflower oil

1 onion, chopped

1 garlic clove, chopped (optional)

2 carrots, chopped

1 lb 2 oz/500 g ground beef

1⅔ cups sliced mushrooms

1¼ cups hot beef stock

1 tsp sugar

1 tbsp Worcestershire sauce

1 cup grated cheddar cheese

salt and pepper

Beef with Garlic Potatoes

1. Preheat the oven to 350°F/180°C. Parboil the potatoes in a pan of salted boiling water for 15 minutes, then drain and let stand until cool enough to handle.

2. Meanwhile, heat 1 tablespoon of the oil in a large pan. Add the onion and cook over low heat, stirring occasionally, for 5 minutes, until softened.

3. Add the ground beef, increase the heat to medium, and cook, stirring frequently and breaking it up with a wooden spoon, for 8–10 minutes, until evenly browned. Add the carrots and tomatoes. Stir the cornstarch into the stock, then stir the mixture into the pan. Season to taste with salt and pepper, stir in the parsley and sage, and bring to a boil. Reduce the heat and simmer for 5 minutes.

4. Meanwhile, cut the potatoes into slices. Combine the garlic and the remaining oil in a small bowl and season to taste with salt and pepper.

5. Transfer the ground beef mixture to an ovenproof dish and arrange the potato slices on top. Brush the garlic-flavored oil over them and bake in the preheated oven for 30–35 minutes, until the topping is golden brown. Serve immediately.

Serves 4

1 lb 2 oz/500 g potatoes
3 tbsp olive oil
* 1 onion, chopped
* 1 lb 2 oz/500 g ground beef
3–4 carrots, chopped
4 tomatoes, peeled and chopped
1 tsp cornstarch
1¼ cups hot beef stock
1 tbsp chopped fresh parsley
1 tsp chopped fresh sage
* 3 garlic cloves, very finely chopped
* salt and pepper

Ground Beef Casserole

1. Heat 2 tablespoons of the oil in a large skillet. Add the ground beef and cook over medium heat, stirring frequently and breaking it up with a wooden spoon, for 8 minutes, until lightly browned. Stir in the scallions, tomatoes, bell pepper, and pineapple and cook, stirring occasionally, for an additional 5 minutes. Stir in the thyme and season to taste with salt and pepper. Reduce the heat and simmer, stirring occasionally, for 15 minutes.

2. Preheat the oven to 350°F/180°C. Heat the remaining oil in a pan. Add the eggplant slices, in batches, and cook for 2–3 minutes on each side, until softened. Add more oil to the pan as required. Remove the eggplant slices from the skillet and drain on paper towels.

3. Put one-third of the eggplant slices in an ovenproof dish and add half the ground beef mixture. Add half the remaining eggplant slices and top with the remaining ground beef mixture. Cover with the remaining eggplant slices, sprinkle with the cheese, and bake in the preheated oven for 30 minutes, until the topping is golden brown. Serve immediately.

Serves 6

6 tbsp olive oil, plus extra if needed

2 lb 4 oz/1 kg ground beef

6 scallions, chopped

6 tomatoes, peeled and chopped

1 red bell pepper, seeded and sliced

2 slices fresh pineapple (about ¾ inch/2 cm thick), peeled, cored, and chopped

1 tbsp chopped fresh thyme

2 eggplants, thinly sliced

1½ cups grated cheddar cheese

salt and pepper

44

Braised Hamburgers

1. Put the ground beef, garlic, shallot, celery, breadcrumbs, basil, and egg into a bowl and season to taste with salt and pepper. Mix well until thoroughly combined, then divide the mixture into 4 equal-size portions and shape them into patties.

2. Heat the oil in a skillet. Add the hamburgers and cook over medium heat for 3 minutes on each side, until browned. Remove from the skillet and keep warm.

3. Add the onion to the skillet and cook over low heat, stirring occasionally, for 5 minutes, until softened. Drain off as much fat as possible. Return the pan to the heat and stir in the stock, then add the bay leaf and season to taste with salt. Return the hamburgers to the skillet and simmer gently for 25 minutes.

4. Transfer the hamburgers to warmed individual plates. Remove and discard the bay leaf, pour the sauce over the hamburgers, and serve immediately.

Serves 4

* 1 lb 7 oz/650 g ground beef
* 2 garlic cloves, finely chopped
* 1 shallot, finely chopped
  1 celery stalk, finely chopped
  ½ cup fresh breadcrumbs
  1 fresh basil sprig, finely chopped
  1 egg, lightly beaten
  2 tbsp sunflower oil
  1 small onion, chopped
  1 cup beef stock
  1 bay leaf
* salt and pepper

Baked Beef & Potato Layers

1. Mix the tomato paste with the water in a bowl, then add to a pan with the tomatoes and thyme. Season to taste with salt and pepper and bring to a boil. Reduce the heat and simmer, stirring occasionally, for 30 minutes, until thickened.

2. Meanwhile, cook the potatoes in a pan of salted boiling water for 20–25 minutes, until tender but not falling apart. Drain and let cool slightly, then cut into ¼-inch/5-mm slices.

3. Preheat the oven to 350°F/180°C. Rub the cut sides of the garlic all over an ovenproof dish, then grease the dish.

4. Combine the ground beef and egg in a bowl and season to taste with salt and pepper. Divide the mixture into 6 portions and shape each into a patty about ¼ inch/5 mm thick. Melt 1 tablespoon of the butter in a skillet. Add the patties and cook over medium heat for 3 minutes on each side, until lightly browned. Remove with a spatula and keep warm. Add the onions to the skillet and cook over low heat, stirring occasionally, for 5 minutes, until softened.

5. Put half the potato slices in the bottom of the prepared dish. Cover with the beef patties, then add the onions and sprinkle with half the cheese. Top with the remaining potato slices and pour over the tomato mixture. Sprinkle with the remaining cheese, dot with the remaining butter, and bake in the preheated oven for 20 minutes. Serve immediately.

Serves 4

scant ¼ cup tomato paste

½ cup water

14 oz/400 g canned chopped tomatoes

1 tbsp chopped fresh thyme

1 lb 2 oz/500 g potatoes

1 garlic clove, halved

8 oz/225 g ground beef

1 egg, lightly beaten

3 tbsp butter, plus extra for greasing

2 onions, sliced

1 cup grated cheddar cheese

salt and pepper

Layered Beef & Feta

1. Heat half the oil in a large skillet. Add the onion and garlic and cook over low heat, stirring occasionally, for 5 minutes, until softened. Add the ground beef, increase the heat to medium, and cook, stirring frequently and breaking up the meat with a wooden spoon, for 8–10 minutes, until evenly browned. Drain off the fat and return the skillet to the heat. Stir in the tomato paste and cook for an additional 2–3 minutes, then stir in the tomatoes, Worcestershire sauce, and oregano. Season to taste with salt and pepper. Reduce the heat, cover, and simmer for 30 minutes.

2. Meanwhile, cook the potatoes in a pan of salted boiling water for 20–25 minutes, until tender but not falling apart. Drain and let cool slightly, then cut into thick slices.

3. Preheat the oven to 350°F/180°C. Brush the eggplant slices with the remaining oil. Heat a large heavy-bottom skillet. Add the eggplant slices, in batches, and cook over medium heat for 3 minutes on each side, until softened. Drain on paper towels.

4. Transfer the ground beef mixture to an ovenproof dish and cover with the potato slices and eggplant slices. Scatter the feta over the top. Mix the yogurt, eggs, and half the Parmesan in a bowl and pour evenly over the dish. Sprinkle with the remaining Parmesan and bake in the preheated oven for 30–35 minutes, until golden brown. Serve immediately.

Serves 6

4 tbsp olive oil
1 onion, chopped
2 garlic cloves, finely chopped
1 lb 7 oz/650 g ground beef
1½ tbsp tomato paste
1 lb 5 oz/600 g canned chopped tomatoes
2 tbsp Worcestershire sauce
1 tbsp chopped fresh oregano
1 lb 10 oz/750 g potatoes
2 eggplants, sliced
1⅓ cups crumbled feta cheese
2½ cups strained plain yogurt
3 extra large eggs, lightly beaten
½ cup grated Parmesan cheese
salt and pepper

47

Beef with Pimientos

1. Heat the oil in a large skillet. Add the onions and garlic, then cook over low heat, stirring occasionally, for 5 minutes, until softened. Add the ground beef, increase the heat to medium, and cook, stirring frequently and breaking up the meat with a wooden spoon, for 8–10 minutes, until evenly browned.

2. Stir in the Worcestershire sauce, lemon juice, paprika, and sugar. Season to taste with salt and pepper, then cook, stirring frequently, for 5 minutes. Add the pimientos, reduce the heat, and simmer, stirring occasionally, for 20 minutes, until the meat is cooked through and tender. Serve immediately.

Serves 4

2 tbsp olive oil

3 large onions, thinly sliced into rings

2 garlic cloves, finely chopped

1 lb 7 oz/650 g ground beef

2 tbsp Worcestershire sauce

3 tbsp lemon juice

1 tsp hot paprika

1 tbsp light brown sugar

4–5 canned pimientos, drained and sliced lengthwise

salt and pepper

Salisbury Casserole

1. Line a 15 x 10-inch/38 x 25-cm ovenproof dish with parchment paper. Put the crackers into a bowl and pour in the water. Let soak for 5 minutes, then add the ground beef and season to taste with salt and pepper. Mix well, then spoon the mixture into the prepared dish, pressing it down well with the back of the spoon. Cover with plastic wrap and chill in the refrigerator for 8 hours or overnight.

2. Preheat the oven to 300°F/150°C. Uncover the dish, cut the ground beef mixture into 12 rectangles, and carefully remove from the dish, using the parchment paper to help you. Remove and discard the parchment paper. Pour the undiluted soup into the dish.

3. Dust the meat rectangles with flour. Heat the oil in a large skillet. Add the rectangles, in batches, and cook for 3–4 minutes on each side, until lightly browned. Remove with a spatula and drain on paper towels, then return to the dish.

4. Bake in the preheated oven for 40–45 minutes, until the meat is tender. Transfer the rectangles to warmed individual plates, spoon the sauce over them, and serve immediately.

Serves 6

2⅔ cups crushed crackers or matzos

1 cup water

3 lb/1.3 kg ground beef

1¼ cups condensed French onion soup

all-purpose flour, for dusting

2 tbsp sunflower oil

salt and pepper

Fried Beef Dumplings

1. Put the ground beef, suet, and onion into a bowl and mix well. Season to taste with salt and pepper, add the spices, and mix well again. Finally, add the egg and mix until thoroughly combined.

2. Break off pieces of the mixture and shape into 2-inch/5-cm balls. Spread out the oats in a shallow dish and roll the dumplings in it until coated.

3. Heat enough oil for deep-frying in a deep-fryer to 350–375°F/180–190°C, or until a cube of bread browns in 30 seconds. Add the dumplings and cook for 8–10 minutes, until golden brown and cooked through.

4. Remove the dumplings and drain well. Transfer to a warmed serving dish and serve immediately with the tomato sauce.

Serves 6

✳ 1 lb 7 oz/650 g ground beef
1½ cups shredded beef suet
✳ 4½ tbsp finely chopped onion
½ tsp ground ginger
¼ tsp ground cloves
¼ tsp ground nutmeg
1 extra large egg, lightly beaten
¾ cup medium oats
vegetable oil, for deep-frying
✳ salt and pepper
1 quantity Tomato Sauce, to serve (see page 58)

50

Beef-Filled Crêpes

1. First, make the crêpe batter. Sift the flour and salt into a bowl, then add the egg and half the milk and beat until smooth. Stir in the remaining milk and the oil. Set aside.

2. Heat the oil in a skillet. Add the onion and carrots and cook over low heat, stirring occasionally, for 5 minutes, until softened. Add the ground beef, increase the heat to medium, and cook, stirring frequently and breaking it up with a wooden spoon, for 8–10 minutes, until evenly browned. Reserve 2 tablespoons of the stock, stir the tomato paste into the remainder, and add to the skillet. Season to taste with salt and pepper, reduce the heat, and simmer, stirring occasionally, for 30 minutes.

3. Meanwhile, preheat the oven to 375°F/190°C. Brush a 10-inch/25-cm crêpe pan with oil and heat. Stir the batter and pour a little into the center of the hot pan, then tilt and rotate the pan to cover the bottom evenly. Cook for 1–1½ minutes, until the underside is golden brown, then flip over the crêpe and cook the other side for 30 seconds. Make more crêpes with the remaining batter, brushing the pan with more oil as required.

4. Mix the flour with the reserved stock and stir into the ground beef mixture. Simmer, stirring constantly, for a few minutes, until thickened. Divide the filling among the crêpes and roll them up. Place in an ovenproof dish in a single layer and bake in the preheated oven for 15 minutes. Serve immediately.

Serves 4

2 tbsp sunflower oil, plus extra
 for brushing
1 onion, chopped
2 carrots, grated
1 lb 2 oz/500 g ground beef
1¼ cups hot beef stock
1 tbsp tomato paste
1 tbsp all-purpose flour
salt and pepper

Crêpe batter
1 cup all-purpose flour
pinch of salt
1 egg, lightly beaten
1¼ cups milk
1 tsp sunflower oil

Beef Potpie

1. Heat the oil in a pan. Add the onions and garlic and cook over low heat, stirring occasionally, for 5 minutes, until softened. Add the ground beef, increase the heat to medium, and cook, stirring frequently and breaking it up with a wooden spoon, for 8–10 minutes, until evenly browned.

2. Add the mushrooms and tomatoes and cook for 3 minutes, then stir in the anchovy essence, Worcestershire sauce, oregano, bay leaf, stock, and wine. Season to taste with salt and pepper. Bring to a boil, then reduce the heat and simmer, stirring occasionally, for 20 minutes.

3. Meanwhile, preheat the oven to 350°F/180°C. Sift the flour and salt into a bowl. Add the butter and rub in with your fingertips until the mixture resembles breadcrumbs. Stir in the cheese. Stir in the egg yolk and enough of the milk to mix to a soft dough. Shape the dough into an 8-inch/20-cm circle.

4. Transfer the ground beef mixture to an 8-inch/20-cm round cake pan and put the dough circle on top. Bake in the preheated oven for 50 minutes, until the topping is golden brown. Remove the pan from the oven and invert onto a warmed serving dish. Cut into wedges and serve immediately.

Serves 4

3 tbsp sunflower oil
2 onions, finely chopped
1 garlic clove, finely chopped
12 oz/350 g ground beef
¾ cup finely chopped mushrooms
4 tomatoes, peeled and diced
1 tsp anchovy essence
1 tbsp Worcestershire sauce
1 tsp dried oregano
1 bay leaf
⅔ cup beef stock
⅔ cup red wine
salt and pepper

Pie dough
1½ cups self-rising flour
pinch of salt
4 tbsp butter
¾ cup grated cheddar cheese
1 egg yolk
½–⅔ cup milk

Beef & Cheese Cobbler

1. Preheat the oven to 350°F/180°C. Heat the oil in a skillet. Add the ground beef and cook over medium heat, stirring frequently and breaking it up with a wooden spoon, for 8–10 minutes, until evenly browned.

2. Remove the skillet from the heat and spoon the ground beef into a casserole, then stir in the all-purpose flour. Add the onions, ketchup, thyme, and bay leaf and season to taste with salt and pepper. Pour in the stock and stir well, then cover and bake in the preheated oven for 1 hour.

3. Meanwhile, make the cobbler topping. Sift the self-rising flour, dry mustard, and salt into a bowl. Add the butter and rub in with your fingertips until the mixture resembles breadcrumbs. Stir in the cheese, Tabasco sauce, and enough water to mix to a soft dough.

4. Roll out the dough to a thickness of ½ inch/1 cm on a lightly floured surface, then stamp out circles with a 6-cm/2½-inch round cutter.

5. Remove the casserole from the oven and take off the lid. Remove and discard the bay leaf. Cover the ground beef mixture with the dough circles and brush them with a little milk. Return the casserole, without the lid, to the oven and bake for an additional 35 minutes, until the topping is golden brown. Serve immediately.

Serves 4

2 tbsp sunflower oil
1 lb 2 oz/500 g ground beef
2 tbsp all-purpose flour
1 lb 2 oz/500 g onions, cut into wedges
2 tbsp ketchup
1 tbsp chopped fresh thyme
1 bay leaf
1¼ cups beef stock
milk, for glazing
salt and pepper

Cobbler topping
2 cups self-rising flour, plus extra for dusting
½ tsp dry mustard
pinch of salt
3 tbsp butter, cut into small pieces
¾ cup grated cheddar cheese
dash of Tabasco sauce

French Meat Tart

① Melt the butter with the oil in a large skillet. Add the onions and garlic and cook over low heat, stirring occasionally, for 5 minutes, until softened. Add the ground beef, increase the heat to medium, and cook, stirring frequently and breaking it up with a wooden spoon, for 5 minutes. Add the bulk sausage and cook, stirring frequently, for an additional 3–5 minutes, until all the meat is evenly browned.

② Mix the tomato paste with the water in a small bowl, then add to the pan with the sage. Season to taste with salt and pepper, reduce the heat, and simmer for 10 minutes. Remove from the heat and let cool.

③ Meanwhile, roll out three-quarters of the dough on a lightly floured surface into a ¼ inch/5 mm thick circle. Lift the dough into a 9-inch/23-cm loose-bottom fluted tart pan, easing it into the bottom and sides. Run the rolling pin over the rim to trim the edges. Chill in the refrigerator for 30 minutes.

④ Preheat the oven to 350°F/180°C. Using a slotted spoon, transfer the ground beef mixture into the pie shell, spreading it evenly. Roll out the remaining dough and cut into ¼ inch/5 mm wide strips. Arrange the strips over the filling in a lattice, then brush with the egg white. Place on a baking sheet and bake in the preheated oven for 40 minutes, until golden. Serve immediately.

Serves 4

2 tbsp butter

2 tbsp olive oil

2 onions, chopped

1 garlic clove, finely chopped

10½ oz/300 g ground beef

10½ oz/300 g bulk sausage or sausage meat removed from the casings

1 tbsp tomato paste

2 tbsp water

1 tsp chopped fresh sage

350 g/12 oz store-bought flaky pie dough, thawed if frozen

all-purpose flour, for dusting

1 egg white, lightly beaten

salt and pepper

Greek Baked Pasta

1. Heat half the oil in a pan. Add the onion and garlic and cook over low heat, stirring occasionally, for 5 minutes, until softened. Add the ground beef, increase the heat to medium, and cook, stirring frequently and breaking it up with a wooden spoon, for 8–10 minutes, until evenly browned. Stir in the strained pureed tomatoes, sugar, vinegar, and parsley and season to taste with salt and pepper. Reduce the heat, cover, and simmer for 15 minutes, until thickened.

2. Meanwhile, preheat the oven to 350°F/180°C. Preheat the broiler. Brush a large ovenproof dish with oil. Bring a large pan of salted water to a boil. Add the macaroni, return to a boil, and cook for 8–10 minutes, until tender but still firm to the bite. Drain and return to the pan. Stir in the remaining oil and the Gruyère.

3. Spread out the eggplant slices on a baking sheet and brush on both sides with oil. Cook under the preheated broiler for 5 minutes on each side, until golden. Line the bottom and sides of the prepared dish with the eggplant slices.

4. Stir the eggs and Parmesan into the béchamel sauce, then stir 3 tablespoons of the mixture into the ground beef mixture. Spoon half the macaroni evenly over the eggplant slices and pour in half the béchamel mixture. Add the ground beef mixture and top with the remaining macaroni. Pour the remaining béchamel mixture over the top. Bake in the preheated oven for 35–40 minutes, until golden brown. Let stand for 10 minutes before serving.

Serves 6

4 tbsp olive oil, plus extra for brushing

1 small onion, finely chopped

2 garlic cloves, finely chopped

1 lb 2 oz/500 g ground beef

2 cups strained pureed tomatoes

1 tsp sugar

2 tsp red wine vinegar

3 tbsp chopped fresh flat-leaf parsley

8 oz/225 g dried macaroni

2 cups grated Gruyère cheese,

2 lb 4 oz/1 kg eggplants, sliced lengthwise

2 eggs, lightly beaten

generous 1 cup grated Parmesan cheese

1 quantity Béchamel Sauce (see page 70)

salt and pepper

Bolognese Soufflé

1. Heat half the oil in a skillet. Add the bacon and cook over low heat, stirring occasionally, for 2–3 minutes. Add the onion and garlic and cook, stirring occasionally, for 5 minutes, until softened. Add the ground beef, increase the heat to medium, and cook, stirring frequently and breaking it up with a wooden spoon, for 5–8 minutes, until evenly browned.

2. Stir in the tomatoes, tomato paste, and thyme and season to taste with salt and pepper. Reduce the heat and simmer for 25 minutes, then remove from the heat and let cool.

3. Meanwhile, bring a pan of salted water to a boil. Add the pasta, return to a boil, and cook for 8–10 minutes, until tender but still firm to the bite. Drain, return to the pan, and toss with the remaining oil. Preheat the oven to 375°F/190°C. Brush a soufflé dish with oil and sprinkle with the Parmesan.

4. Beat the egg yolks into the cooled ground beef mixture and fold in the pasta. Stiffly whisk the egg whites in a grease-free bowl, then fold into the beef-and-pasta mixture. Gently spoon into the prepared dish and bake in the preheated oven for 45 minutes, until risen and golden brown. Serve immediately.

Serves 4

2 tbsp olive oil, plus extra for brushing

4 bacon slices, finely chopped

1 large onion, finely chopped

1 garlic clove, finely chopped

10½ oz/300 g ground beef

14 oz/400 g canned chopped tomatoes

1 tbsp tomato paste

1 tbsp chopped fresh thyme

6 oz/175 g dried penne

⅓ cup grated Parmesan cheese

3 eggs, separated

salt and pepper

56

Hamburgers with Beet

1. Heat 1 tablespoon of the oil in a skillet. Add the onion and cook over low heat, stirring occasionally, for 5 minutes, until softened.

2. Transfer the onion to a large bowl and add the ground beef, egg, vinegar, paprika, and capers and mix well with your hands. Add the beet and sour cream, season to taste with salt and pepper, and mix well again. Shape the mixture into 4 patties.

3. Melt 2 tablespoons of the butter with the remaining oil in a skillet. Add the hamburgers and cook over medium heat for 6–7 minutes on each side, until well browned. Remove with a spatula and drain on paper towels.

4. Melt half the remaining butter in a skillet. Break 2 eggs into separate cups and slide them into the skillet. Immediately collect the whites around the yolks with a spatula to keep them neat and separated and cook for a few minutes, until the whites have set but the yolks are still runny. Cook the remaining eggs in the remaining butter in the same way. Transfer the burgers to a warmed serving dish, top with the fried eggs, and serve immediately.

Serves 4

3 tbsp sunflower oil

1 onion, finely chopped

1 lb 7 oz/650 g ground beef

1 medium egg, lightly beaten

2 tsp white wine vinegar

½ tsp paprika

1 tbsp finely chopped capers

3 tbsp finely chopped cooked beet

2 tbsp sour cream

4 tbsp butter

4 eggs

salt and pepper

Beef & Cheese Roll

1. Tear the bread into pieces, put it into a large bowl with the milk, and let soak for 5 minutes. Squeeze out the excess milk from the bread and pour it off, reserving the soaked bread.

2. Meanwhile, lightly dust a sheet of wax paper with flour. Add the ground beef, onion, dry mustard, parsley, and eggs to the bowl with the bread. Season to taste with salt and pepper and mix well until thoroughly combined. Transfer the mixture to the wax paper, shaping it into a neat rectangle, measuring about 8 x 10 inches/20 x 25 cm. Cover with a second sheet of wax paper and chill in the refrigerator for 1 hour.

3. Preheat the oven to 350°F/180°C. Remove the ground beef mixture from the refrigerator and discard the top sheet of wax paper. Cover the surface with the mozzarella slices, then roll up, starting at a narrow edge and using the paper to help.

4. Carefully transfer the roll to a shallow ovenproof dish or baking pan, placing it seam-side down, and brush with the melted butter. Bake in the preheated oven for 45–50 minutes, until golden brown and cooked through. Serve immediately with the tomato sauce.

Serves 4

3½ slices thick white bread, crusts removed

4 tbsp milk

all-purpose flour, for dusting

1 lb 7 oz/650 g ground beef

1 onion, finely chopped

2 tsp dry mustard

2 tbsp finely chopped fresh parsley

2 eggs, lightly beaten

8 oz/225 g mozzarella cheese, thinly sliced

2 tbsp melted butter

salt and pepper

1 quantity Tomato Sauce, to serve (see page 58)

Meal-in-a-Bowl Beef & Herb Soup

1. Grate 1 of the onions into a bowl and finely chop the other. Heat the oil in a large pan. Add the chopped onion and cook over low–medium heat, stirring occasionally, for 8–10 minutes, until golden. Stir in the turmeric and cumin, add the split peas, and pour in the stock. Bring to a boil, then reduce the heat, cover, and simmer for 15 minutes.

2. Meanwhile, add the ground beef to the grated onion, season to taste with salt and pepper, and mix well. Shape the mixture into small balls with your hands.

3. Add the meatballs to the soup, re-cover the pan, and simmer for an additional 10 minutes. Add the rice and stir in the cilantro, chives, and spinach. Simmer, stirring frequently, for 25–30 minutes, until the rice is tender.

4. Melt the butter in a skillet. Add the garlic and cook over low heat, stirring frequently, for 2–3 minutes. Stir in the mint and cook for an additional minute.

5. Transfer the soup to warmed bowls and sprinkle over the garlic mixture. Serve immediately with yogurt.

Serves 6

- 2 onions
- 2 tbsp sunflower oil
- 1 tbsp ground turmeric
- 1 tsp ground cumin
- scant ½ cup green or yellow split peas
- 5 cups beef stock
- 8 oz/225 g ground beef
- 1 cup long-grain rice
- 1 tbsp chopped fresh cilantro
- 1 tbsp snipped fresh chives
- ⅔ cup finely chopped baby spinach
- 2 tbsp butter
- 2 garlic cloves, finely chopped
- 3 tbsp chopped fresh mint
- salt and pepper
- strained plain yogurt, to serve

59

Dutch Crêpe Cake

1. First, make the batter. Sift the flour and salt into a bowl, then add the egg, egg yolk, and 1 tablespoon of the milk and stir, gradually incorporating the dry ingredients and adding half the remaining milk. When the mixture is thick and smooth, beat in the remaining milk with a whisk. Set aside.

2. Meanwhile, melt the butter in a skillet. Add the onions and cook over low–medium heat, stirring occasionally, for 8–10 minutes, until golden. Add the ground beef and cook, stirring frequently and breaking it up with a wooden spoon, for 8–10 minutes, until evenly browned. Add the mushrooms and cook for an additional 5 minutes, then drain off as much fat as possible. Stir in the parsley and cream and season to taste with salt and pepper. Reduce the heat, cover, and simmer, stirring occasionally, for 20 minutes.

3. Heat a large skillet, then add half the melted butter. Stir the batter and pour half into the hot skillet, then tilt and rotate the skillet to cover the bottom evenly. Cook for 2 minutes, until the underside is golden brown, then flip over the crêpe and cook on the other side for 2 minutes. Slide onto a warmed plate.

4. Add the remaining melted butter to the skillet and pour in the remaining batter. Cook for 3 minutes, then flip over and spoon the ground beef mixture on top of the crêpe. Top with the first crêpe and slide onto a warmed plate. Garnish with parsley, cut into wedges, and serve immediately.

Serves 4

2 tbsp butter
2 onions, finely chopped
1 lb 7 oz/650 g ground beef
1¼ cups thinly sliced mushrooms
2 tbsp chopped fresh parsley, plus extra to garnish
⅔ cup heavy cream
1 tbsp melted butter
salt and pepper

Crêpe batter
1 cup all-purpose flour
pinch of salt
1 egg
1 egg yolk
½ cup milk

60

Beef & Vegetable Gratin

1. Heat the oil in a large pan. Add the garlic and onions and cook over low heat, stirring occasionally, for 8–10 minutes, until golden brown. Add the ground beef, increase the heat to medium, and cook, stirring frequently and breaking it up with a wooden spoon, for 8–10 minutes, until evenly browned. Stir in the zucchini, carrots, bell pepper, and raisins and season to taste with salt and pepper. Reduce the heat, cover, and simmer for 25 minutes, until the vegetables are tender.

2. Meanwhile, preheat the oven to 350°F/180°C. Melt the butter in a separate pan. Add the flour and cook over low heat, stirring constantly, for 2 minutes. Remove the pan from the heat and gradually stir in the milk, a little at a time, until smooth. Return the pan to the heat and bring to a boil, stirring constantly, then cook, stirring, for an additional few minutes, until thickened. Remove the pan from the heat and stir in the cheese until melted.

3. Stir the corn, beans, and parsley into the ground beef mixture and simmer for an additional 3 minutes, then remove the pan from the heat. Spoon into an ovenproof dish.

4. Lightly beat the egg yolks in a bowl with a fork, then stir in 4 tablespoons of the cheese sauce. Stir the egg yolk mixture into the cheese sauce and pour it over the ground beef mixture to cover. Bake in the preheated oven for 25–30 minutes, until the topping is golden brown. Serve immediately.

Serves 6–8

3 tbsp sunflower oil
2 garlic cloves, finely chopped
2 onions, sliced
2 lb 4 oz/1 kg ground beef
1 lb 2 oz/500 g zucchini, thinly sliced
4–5 carrots, thinly sliced
1 red bell pepper, seeded and thinly sliced
generous 1/3 cup raisins
6 tbsp butter
3/4 cup all-purpose flour
3 3/4 cups milk
1 cup grated cheddar cheese
12 oz/350 g canned corn kernels, drained
14 oz/400 g canned cannellini beans, drained and rinsed
2 tbsp chopped fresh parsley
4 egg yolks
salt and pepper

61

Beef & Spinach Cannelloni

1. Cook the spinach, in just the water clinging to the leaves after washing, for 5–8 minutes, until tender, then drain and squeeze out as much liquid as possible. Chop finely.

2. Melt 1 tablespoon of the butter with the oil in a large skillet. Add the shallots and garlic and cook over low heat, stirring occasionally, for 5 minutes, until softened. Add the ground beef, increase the heat to medium, and cook, stirring frequently and breaking it up with a wooden spoon, for 8–10 minutes, until evenly browned. Add the spinach and cook for 3–4 minutes. Transfer the mixture to a bowl, stir in 3 tablespoons of the Parmesan, 1½ tablespoons of the cream, the egg, and oregano. Season to taste with salt and pepper.

3. Preheat the oven to 375°F/190°C. Melt 2 tablespoons of the remaining butter in a pan, then stir in the flour and cook, stirring constantly, for 2 minutes. Remove the pan from the heat and gradually stir in the milk and the remaining cream, until smooth. Return the pan to the heat and bring to a boil, stirring constantly. Remove from the heat.

4. Fill the cannelloni tubes with the ground beef mixture. Pour a little of the tomato sauce over the bottom of an ovenproof dish, then put the cannelloni in the dish in 2 layers. Spoon the white sauce over them and top with the remaining tomato sauce. Sprinkle with the remaining Parmesan and dot with the remaining butter. Bake in the preheated oven for 30 minutes. Serve immediately.

Serves 4

2 cups spinach, coarse stalks removed

4 tbsp butter

1½ tbsp olive oil

2 shallots, finely chopped

2 garlic cloves, finely chopped

8 oz/225 g ground beef

1⅓ cups finely grated Parmesan cheese

4½ tbsp heavy cream

1 egg, lightly beaten

pinch of dried oregano

4 tbsp all-purpose flour

¾ cup milk

16 cannelloni tubes, cooked according to package directions

1 quantity Tomato Sauce (see page 58)

salt and pepper

Spicy

62

Taco Soup

1. Heat the oil in a large pan. Add the onion and cook over low heat, stirring occasionally, for 5 minutes, until softened. Add the ground beef, increase the heat to medium, and cook, stirring frequently and breaking it up with a wooden spoon, for 8–10 minutes. Drain off as much fat as possible.

2. Stir in the tomatoes, kidney beans with their can juices, tomato juice, sugar, spices, and stock and bring to a boil. Reduce the heat, cover, and simmer, stirring occasionally, for 15 minutes.

3. Meanwhile, put the cheese, tortilla chips, and sour cream into separate serving dishes. Peel, pit, and dice the avocado and gently toss with the lemon juice.

4. Remove the soup from the heat and ladle into warmed bowls. Scatter the avocado over the soup and serve immediately with the cheese, tortilla chips, and sour cream.

Serves 4–6

1 tbsp sunflower oil

1 small onion, finely chopped

8 oz/225 g ground beef

14 oz/400 g canned chopped tomatoes

14 oz/400 g canned red kidney beans

1 cup tomato juice

1 tsp sugar

¼ tsp ground cinnamon

¼ tsp ground cumin

1 tsp chili powder

1½ cups beef stock

1 cup coarsely grated Monterey Jack or cheddar cheese

12 oz/350 g tortilla chips

1 cup sour cream

1 avocado

2 tbsp lemon juice

63

Chili Burgers

1. Preheat the broiler. Combine the onion, breadcrumbs, cilantro, chili powder, garlic salt, cumin, and milk in a bowl. Add the ground beef and mix well with your hands until thoroughly combined.

2. Divide the mixture into 4 portions and shape into hamburgers. Cook under the preheated broiler for 5–8 minutes on each side, until cooked to your liking.

3. Spread the bottom of each bun with guacamole and top with the lettuce leaves, burgers, and tomato slices. Cover with the tops of the buns. Serve immediately with tortilla chips.

Serves 4

* 1 small onion, finely chopped
1 cup fresh breadcrumbs
2 tbsp chopped fresh cilantro
½ tsp chili powder or cayenne pepper
½ tsp garlic salt
1 tsp ground cumin
generous ⅓ cup milk
* 2 lb 4 oz/1 kg ground beef

To serve
4 hamburger buns, split and toasted
guacamole
lettuce leaves
tomato slices
tortilla chips

Enchiladas

1. Heat 1 tablespoon of the oil in a skillet. Add three-quarters of the onions and half the garlic and cook over low heat, stirring occasionally, for 5 minutes. Add the ground beef, increase the heat to medium, and cook, stirring frequently and breaking it up with a wooden spoon, for 8–10 minutes, until evenly browned. Remove the skillet from the heat and transfer the mixture to a bowl. Stir in the cheese and three-quarters of the chiles and season to taste with salt and pepper.

2. Heat the remaining oil in a pan. Add the remaining onion, garlic, and chile and cook over medium heat, stirring occasionally, for 7–8 minutes. Stir in the tomatoes, tomato paste, oregano, Tabasco sauce, and sugar. Season to taste with salt and cook for an additional 3 minutes. Stir in the cream, then reduce the heat, cover, and simmer, stirring occasionally, for 15 minutes. Remove from the heat and let cool slightly.

3. Meanwhile, preheat the oven to 350°F/180°C. Heat a skillet and brush with oil. One at a time, dip the tortillas in the tomato sauce, shake off any excess, and cook for 30 seconds on each side. Transfer to a large plate, put a tablespoon of the ground beef mixture in the center, and roll up. Put the filled tortillas in a large ovenproof dish and pour the remaining tomato sauce over them. Sprinkle with the Parmesan and bake in the preheated oven for 15–20 minutes. Serve immediately.

Serves 6

4 tbsp corn oil, plus extra for brushing

2 onions, finely chopped

2 garlic cloves, finely chopped

8 oz/225 g ground beef

½ cup grated cheddar cheese

4 fresh red chiles, seeded and finely chopped

14 oz/400 g canned chopped tomatoes

scant ½ cup tomato paste

pinch of dried oregano

dash of Tabasco sauce

1 tsp sugar

½ cup heavy cream

18 flour or corn tortillas

2 tbsp grated Parmesan cheese

salt and pepper

Chili con Carne

1. Heat the oil in a large pan. Add the onions and garlic and cook over low heat, stirring occasionally, for 5 minutes, until softened. Add the ground beef, increase the heat to medium, and cook, stirring frequently and breaking it up with a wooden spoon, for 8–10 minutes, until evenly browned.

2. Stir in the tomatoes, tomato paste, cumin, cayenne pepper, chili powder, oregano, bay leaf, and stock. Season to taste with salt. Bring to a boil, then reduce the heat, cover, and simmer, stirring occasionally, for 1 hour.

3. Add the kidney beans, re-cover the pan, and simmer, stirring occasionally, for an additional 30 minutes. Remove and discard the bay leaf. Serve immediately with rice.

Serves 6

2 tbsp corn oil

2 onions, thinly sliced

2 garlic cloves, finely chopped

1 lb 7 oz/650 g ground beef

7 oz/200 g canned chopped tomatoes

5 tbsp tomato paste

1 tsp ground cumin

1 tsp cayenne pepper

1 tbsp chili powder

1 tsp dried oregano

1 bay leaf

1½ cups beef stock

14 oz/400 g canned red kidney beans, drained and rinsed

salt

cooked rice, to serve

66

Fiery Beef Tacos

1. Heat the oil in a skillet. Add the onion and garlic and cook over low heat, stirring occasionally, for 5 minutes, until softened. Add the ground beef, increase the heat to medium, and cook, stirring frequently and breaking it up with a wooden spoon, for 8–10 minutes, until evenly browned. Drain off as much fat as possible.

2. Stir in the chili powder and cumin, season to taste with salt and pepper, and cook over low heat, stirring frequently for 8 minutes, then remove from the heat.

3. Heat the taco shells according to the package directions. Meanwhile, peel, pit, and slice the avocado and gently toss with the lemon juice in a bowl.

4. Divide the lettuce, scallions, tomatoes, and avocado slices among the taco shells. Add a tablespoon of sour cream to each, then divide the ground beef mixture among them. Sprinkle with the cheese and serve immediately.

Serves 4

2 tbsp corn oil
1 small onion, finely chopped
2 garlic cloves, finely chopped
10 oz/280 g ground beef
1½ tsp hot chili powder
1 tsp ground cumin
8 taco shells
1 avocado
2 tbsp lemon juice
¼ head of lettuce, shredded
4 scallions, thinly sliced
2 tomatoes, peeled and diced
½ cup sour cream
1 cup grated cheddar cheese
salt and pepper

Burritos

① Soak the beans overnight in a bowl of cold water, then drain. Put the beans into a large pan and pour in water to cover. Bring to a boil and boil vigorously for 15 minutes, then drain, rinse, and return to the pan. Add fresh water to cover and bring to a boil. Reduce the heat, cover, and simmer for 1–1½ hours, until tender, then drain.

② Heat the oil in a large pan. Add the onion, garlic, and bell pepper and cook over low heat, stirring occasionally, for 5 minutes, until softened. Add the ground beef, increase the heat to medium, and cook, stirring frequently and breaking it up with a wooden spoon, for 8–10 minutes, until evenly browned. Reduce the heat, stir in the spices, oregano, and ketchup, and season to taste with salt. Add the wine, tomatoes, bay leaf, and beans and mix well. Cover and simmer, stirring occasionally, for 25 minutes. Stir in the jalapeño chiles and cilantro and remove from the heat. Remove and discard the bay leaf.

③ Meanwhile, preheat the oven to 350°F/180°C. Brush a large ovenproof dish with oil. Using a slotted spoon, divide the ground beef mixture among the tortillas and roll up. Put them in the prepared dish, seam-side down, and sprinkle with the cheese. Bake in the preheated oven for 15 minutes. Serve immediately with guacamole and salsa.

Serves 6

8 oz/225 g dried black beans

2 tbsp vegetable oil, plus extra for brushing

1 Bermuda onion, chopped

2 garlic cloves, finely chopped

1 red bell pepper, seeded and chopped

1 lb 4 oz/550 g ground beef

1 tbsp ground cumin

1 tsp paprika

¼ tsp cayenne pepper

pinch of dried oregano

2 tbsp ketchup

scant ½ cup red wine

14 oz/400 g canned chopped tomatoes

1 bay leaf

3 tbsp chopped pickled jalapeño chiles

1 tbsp chopped fresh cilantro

12 flour tortillas

⅔ cup grated cheddar cheese

salt

guacamole and salsa, to serve

Empanadas

1. Heat the oil in a large skillet. Add the onion, garlic, and bell pepper and cook over low heat, stirring occasionally, for 5 minutes. Add the ground beef, increase the heat to medium, and cook, stirring frequently and breaking it up with a wooden spoon, for 8–10 minutes, until evenly browned. Drain off as much fat as possible.

2. Stir the tomatoes, raisins, chili powder, and cumin into the skillet. Season to taste with salt and pepper, reduce the heat, and simmer for 10 minutes. Remove the skillet from the heat.

3. Meanwhile, preheat the oven to 375°F/190°C. Brush a large baking sheet with oil. Roll out the dough on a lightly floured surface and stamp out 8 circles with a 5-inch/13-cm plain cutter. Put a tablespoon of the ground beef mixture on 1 side of each dough circle, brush the edges with water, and fold over. Press the edges with a fork or your finger to seal.

4. Transfer to the prepared baking sheet and bake in the preheated oven for 30–35 minutes, until golden brown. Serve immediately.

Makes 8

2 tbsp corn oil, plus extra for brushing

1 onion, finely chopped

1 garlic clove, finely chopped

½ small red bell pepper, seeded and diced

8 oz/225 g ground beef

2 tomatoes, peeled and diced

scant ½ cup raisins

½–1 tsp chili powder

pinch of ground cumin

10½ oz/300 g store-bought puff pastry, thawed if frozen

all-purpose flour, for dusting

salt and pepper

69

Nachos

1. Preheat the oven to 350°F/180°C. Heat the oil in a large skillet. Add the onion and garlic, if using, and cook over low heat, stirring occasionally, for 5 minutes, until softened. Add the ground beef, increase the heat to medium, and cook, stirring frequently and breaking it up with a wooden spoon, for 8–10 minutes, until evenly browned. Remove from the heat, drain off as much fat as possible, and season to taste with salt and pepper.

2. Spread out the tortilla chips in a large ovenproof dish and spoon the refried beans evenly over them. Sprinkle with half the cheese, cover with the ground beef mixture, and top with the remaining cheese. Sprinkle with the jalapeño chiles and bake in the preheated oven for 10–15 minutes, until the cheese has melted. Serve immediately with sour cream, guacamole, and salsa.

Serves 4–6

1 tbsp corn oil

* 1 onion, finely chopped

* 1 garlic clove, finely chopped (optional)

* 1 lb 2 oz/500 g ground beef

1 lb/450 g tortilla chips

14 oz/400 g canned refried beans

2 cups coarsely grated Monterey Jack or cheddar cheese

4 tbsp chopped pickled jalapeño chiles

* salt and pepper

sour cream, guacamole, and salsa, to serve

Mexican Beef Stew

1. Heat the oil in a large pan. Add the onion, garlic, and bell pepper and cook over low heat, stirring occasionally, for 5 minutes. Add the ground beef, increase the heat to medium, and cook, stirring frequently and breaking it up with a wooden spoon, for 8–10 minutes, until evenly browned.

2. Stir in the chiles, cumin seeds, cilantro, corn, kidney beans, tomato paste, and stock and season to taste with salt and pepper. Reduce the heat, cover, and simmer, stirring occasionally, for 50–60 minutes. Serve immediately.

Serves 4

2 tbsp corn oil

1 onion, finely chopped

2 garlic cloves, finely chopped

1 green bell pepper, seeded and finely chopped

1 lb 2 oz/500 g ground beef

3 fresh green chiles, seeded and finely chopped

1 tsp cumin seeds, lightly toasted

1 tbsp chopped fresh cilantro

5 oz/140 g canned corn kernels, drained

7 oz/200 g canned red kidney beans, drained and rinsed

1 tbsp tomato paste

2 cups beef stock

salt and pepper

Beef Tamale

1. Heat the oil in a large skillet. Add the onion and cook over low heat, stirring occasionally, for 5 minutes, until softened. Add the ground beef, increase the heat to medium, and cook, stirring frequently and breaking it up with the spoon, for 8–10 minutes, until evenly browned.

2. Stir in the ham, capers, golden raisins, olives, tomato paste, chili powder, thyme, and sugar and season to taste with salt and pepper. Reduce the heat and simmer, stirring frequently, for 5 minutes. Stir in the corn, then remove the pan from the heat and stir in the eggs.

3. Cut four 6-inch/15-cm squares of double layer wax paper. Divide the mixture among them and gather together the edges to seal. Put them into a steamer set over a pan of boiling water, cover, and steam for 45–50 minutes. Remove from the steamer and serve immediately.

Serves 4

2 tbsp corn oil

1 large onion, finely chopped

1 lb/450 g ground beef

1 cup finely diced ham

1 tbsp drained capers

4 tbsp golden raisins

1 tbsp chopped pitted green olives

4 tbsp tomato paste

1/4–1/2 tsp chili powder

2 tsp chopped fresh thyme

1 tsp sugar

11 1/2 oz/325 g canned corn kernels, drained

3 eggs, lightly beaten

salt and pepper

72

Spicy Beef & Sweet Potatoes

1. Preheat the oven to 400°F/200°C. Prick the sweet potatoes all over with a fork. Put them directly on an oven shelf and bake in the preheated oven for 1 hour, until soft.

2. Meanwhile, put the tomatoes, chiles, peppercorns, allspice berries, cinnamon stick, and coriander into a pan and bring to a boil. Reduce the heat and simmer, stirring occasionally, for 30 minutes, until thickened. Remove the pan from the heat and discard the cinnamon stick, then press the sauce through a nylon strainer into a bowl.

3. Heat half the oil in a skillet. Add the ground beef and cook over medium heat, stirring frequently and breaking it up with a wooden spoon, for 8–10 minutes, until evenly browned. Stir in the tomato mixture and tomato paste and season to taste with salt. Simmer, stirring frequently, for 20 minutes.

4. Remove the sweet potatoes from the oven. When they are cool enough to handle, peel off the skins and chop the flesh.

5. Heat the remaining oil in a skillet. Add the onion and garlic and cook over low heat, stirring occasionally, for 5 minutes, until softened. Add the sweet potatoes and stock and cook, stirring constantly, for 5 minutes. Season to taste with salt, remove from the heat, and transfer the mixture to a warmed serving dish. Top with the ground beef mixture and serve immediately with the sour cream.

Serves 4

4 sweet potatoes

1 lb 12 oz/800 g canned chopped tomatoes

2 fresh green chiles, seeded and chopped

6 black peppercorns

6 allspice berries

1 cinnamon stick

1 tsp ground coriander

2 tbsp sunflower oil

1 lb 7 oz/650 g ground beef

1 tbsp tomato paste

1 onion, finely chopped

1 garlic clove, finely chopped

4 tbsp beef stock

½ cup sour cream

salt

Spicy Ground Beef Casserole

1. Preheat the oven to 350°F/180°C. Grease an 11-cup ovenproof dish. Tear the bread into pieces, put it into a bowl with the milk, and let soak.

2. Melt the butter with the oil in a skillet. Add the onions and garlic and cook over medium heat, stirring occasionally, for 8–10 minutes, until lightly browned. Remove from the heat and transfer the onions and garlic to a bowl. Sprinkle in the curry powder and add the ground beef, golden raisins, slivered almonds, parsley, lemon juice, vinegar, and sugar. Season to taste with salt and pepper. Mix well until thoroughly combined, then squeeze out the bread, reserving the milk, and stir the bread into the mixture. Lightly beat 1 of the eggs and stir it into the mixture, then transfer to the prepared dish, pressing it down well.

3. Pour the reserved milk into a measuring cup and make it up to ¾ cup if necessary, then beat in the remaining egg. Pour over the ground beef mixture.

4. Stand the dish in a roasting pan and pour in boiling water to come about halfway up the side. Bake in the preheated oven for 1 hour, until the topping is golden brown. Serve immediately.

Serves 4–6

3 thick slices white bread, crusts removed

1¼ cups milk, plus extra if needed

4 tbsp butter, plus extra for greasing

1 tbsp sunflower oil

2 onions, chopped

1 garlic clove, finely chopped

1½ tbsp curry powder

2 lb 4 oz/1 kg ground beef

generous ¾ cup golden raisins

½ cup slivered almonds

1 tbsp chopped fresh parsley

2 tbsp lemon juice

1 tbsp white wine vinegar

1 tbsp sugar

2 eggs

salt and pepper

Indonesian Beef Parcels

1. Put the shallots, garlic, ground beef, cumin, coriander, and curry powder into a bowl, season to taste with salt and pepper, and mix well until combined. Heat a wok over a medium heat, add the ground beef mixture, and cook, stirring constantly, for 8–10 minutes, until the meat is evenly browned. Remove from the heat and let cool, then stir in just enough of the beaten egg to bind, reserving the remainder.

2. Preheat the oven to 400°F/200°C. Lightly dust a baking sheet with flour. Brush 1 sheet of dough with oil, put a second sheet on top, and cut the double layer in half. Put a spoonful of the ground beef mixture in the center of each piece and fold the sides into the center. Brush the edges with beaten egg and fold the top and bottom into the center. Put the parcels on the prepared baking sheet and place in the refrigerator while you make more parcels in the same way.

3. Brush the tops of the parcels with beaten egg and bake in the preheated oven for 20 minutes, until golden brown. Transfer to a warmed serving dish and serve immediately.

Makes 16

* 4 shallots, finely chopped
* 2 garlic cloves, finely chopped
* 1 lb 2 oz/500 g ground beef
  1 tsp ground cumin
  1 tsp ground coriander
  2 tsp curry powder
  2–3 eggs, lightly beaten
  all-purpose flour, for dusting
  16 sheets filo dough
  peanut oil, for brushing
* salt and pepper

75

Curry Puffs

1. Heat the oil in a skillet. Add the onion, garlic, ginger, and chiles and cook over low heat, stirring occasionally, for 5 minutes, until softened. Stir in the chili powder, coriander, and turmeric, season to taste with salt, and cook, stirring occasionally, for an additional 3 minutes.

2. Add the ground beef, increase the heat to medium, and cook, stirring frequently and breaking it up with a wooden spoon, for 8–10 minutes, until evenly browned. Stir in the tomato, peas, and lime juice, reduce the heat, and cook, stirring occasionally, for an additional 5 minutes. Remove the skillet from the heat.

3. Preheat the oven to 400°F/200°C. Roll out the dough on a lightly floured surface to a thickness of about ⅛ inch/3 mm. Stamp out 20 circles with a 4-inch/10-cm cutter.

4. Put 2 teaspoons of the ground beef mixture on 1 side of each dough circle, brush the edges with water, and fold over. Press the edges with a fork or your finger to seal. Transfer to a baking sheet, brush with beaten egg, and bake in the preheated oven for 20–30 minutes, until golden brown. Remove from the oven, transfer to a wire rack, and let cool slightly. Serve warm.

Makes 20

2 tbsp peanut oil
* 1 onion, finely chopped
* 1 garlic clove, finely chopped
½-inch/1-cm piece fresh ginger, finely chopped
2 fresh red chiles, seeded and finely chopped
1 tsp chili powder
½ tsp ground coriander
½ tsp ground turmeric
* 8 oz/225 g ground beef
1 tomato, peeled and diced
½ cup frozen peas, thawed
2 tbsp lime juice
1 lb 2 oz/500 g store-bought puff pastry, thawed if frozen
all-purpose flour, for dusting
1 egg, lightly beaten
* salt

Indian Kabobs

1. Put the onion, garlic, ginger, chiles, turmeric, cilantro, yogurt, lemon juice, ground beef, and breadcrumbs into a bowl. Season to taste with salt and mix well with your hands until thoroughly combined. Cover with plastic wrap and let rest at room temperature for 30 minutes.

2. Preheat the broiler and brush 12 metal or presoaked wooden skewers with melted butter. Damp your hands and shape small quantities of the ground beef mixture into 24 cigar shapes. Thread 2 onto each skewer and put them in the broiler pan.

3. Brush with melted butter and cook under the preheated broiler for 5 minutes. Turn the skewers, brush with more melted butter, and cook for an additional 4 minutes, until the kabobs are cooked through and browned.

4. Transfer the kabobs to a warmed serving dish, drizzle with yogurt, and garnish with cilantro. Serve immediately with tomato-and-onion salad and naan.

Serves 4

* 1 onion, finely chopped
* 2 garlic cloves, finely chopped
* 1½-inch/4-cm piece fresh ginger, finely chopped
* 2 fresh green chiles, seeded and finely chopped
* ½ tsp ground turmeric
* 2 tbsp chopped fresh cilantro, plus extra to garnish
* 3 tbsp plain yogurt, plus extra to serve
* 1 tbsp lemon juice
* 1 lb 7 oz/650 g ground beef
* 4 tbsp fresh breadcrumbs
* melted butter, for brushing
* salt
* tomato-and-onion salad and warm naan, to serve

Beef Curry

1. Heat the oil in a skillet. Add the onions, garlic, and ginger and cook over low heat, stirring occasionally, for 5 minutes, until softened. Add the coriander, chili powder, and turmeric and cook, stirring occasionally, for an additional 3 minutes.

2. Add the ground beef, increase the heat to medium, and cook, stirring frequently and breaking it up with a wooden spoon, for 8–10 minutes, until evenly browned. Stir in the tomatoes and season to taste with salt. Reduce the heat, cover, and simmer, stirring occasionally, for 15 minutes. Uncover the pan and cook for an additional 5 minutes.

3. Taste and adjust the seasoning, adding salt if needed. Transfer the curry to a warmed serving dish, sprinkle with the cilantro, and serve immediately with rice.

Serves 4

3 tbsp corn oil

4 onions, thinly sliced

2 garlic cloves, finely chopped

1-inch/2.5-cm piece fresh ginger, finely chopped

1 tsp ground coriander

1 tsp chili powder

1 tsp ground turmeric

1 lb 7 oz/650 g ground beef

7 oz/200 g canned chopped tomatoes

2 tbsp chopped fresh cilantro

salt

cooked rice, to serve

78

Indian Potato Cakes

1. Cook the potatoes in a large pan of salted boiling water for 20–25 minutes, until tender but not falling apart. Drain, return to the pan, and mash well.

2. Heat 1 tablespoon of the oil in a large skillet. Add the onion, garlic, chiles, ginger, cumin, coriander, mint, and cilantro and cook over low heat, stirring occasionally, for 5 minutes. Add the ground beef, increase the heat to medium, and cook, stirring frequently and breaking it up with a wooden spoon, for 5 minutes. Add the peas and cook, stirring frequently, for an additional 3–5 minutes, until the meat is evenly browned and the mixture is dry. Remove from the heat, season to taste with salt, and stir in the lemon juice.

3. Divide the mashed potatoes into 10 pieces. Put 1 in your hand and flatten it into a circle. Put a spoonful of the ground beef mixture in the middle and reshape to enclose the filling completely. Make 9 more potato cakes in the same way.

4. Lightly beat the eggs in a shallow dish. Spread out the breadcrumbs in a separate shallow dish. Dip the potato cakes first in the beaten egg and then in the breadcrumbs to coat. Chill in the refrigerator for 30 minutes.

5. Heat the remaining oil in a skillet. Add the potato cakes, in batches, and cook over medium heat, turning occasionally, until golden brown all over. Serve immediately.

Makes 10

2 lb 4 oz/1 kg potatoes, cut into chunks

scant ½ cup peanut oil

1 large onion, finely chopped

2 garlic cloves, finely chopped

2 fresh green chiles, seeded and finely chopped

1½-inch/4-cm piece fresh ginger, finely chopped

1 tsp ground cumin

1 tsp ground coriander

2 tbsp chopped fresh mint

1 tbsp chopped fresh cilantro

8 oz/225 g ground beef

½ cup frozen peas, thawed

4 tbsp lemon juice

2 eggs

2 cups fresh breadcrumbs

salt

Beef Samosas

1. For the dough, sift the flour and salt into a bowl and make a well in the center. Pour the oil into the well and add the lukewarm water. Gradually incorporate the dry ingredients into the liquid, adding a little more warm water if necessary. Turn out onto a lightly floured surface and knead until smooth and elastic. Shape into a ball and let rest for 30 minutes.

2. Meanwhile, heat the oil in a large skillet. Add the onion, garlic, and ginger and cook over low heat, stirring occasionally, for 5 minutes, until softened. Stir in the chili powder, turmeric, coriander, and garam masala and cook, stirring occasionally, for 3 minutes. Add the ground beef, increase the heat to medium, and cook, stirring frequently and breaking it up with a wooden spoon, for 8–10 minutes, until evenly browned. Remove from the heat, stir in the lemon juice and mint, and let cool.

3. Divide the dough into 14 pieces. Roll out each piece into an oval about 8 inches/20 cm long, then cut in half widthwise. Brush the straight edge of 1 piece with water and fold in each side to make a cone. Put a generous tablespoonful of the beef mixture into the cone, brush the open side with water, and press to seal. Make 27 more samosas in the same way.

4. Heat enough oil for deep-frying in a deep-fryer to 350–375°F/180–190°C, or until a cube of bread browns in 30 seconds. Add the samosas, in batches, and cook until crisp and golden brown. Serve immediately with chili sauce.

Makes 28

2 tbsp sunflower oil, plus extra for deep-frying
1 onion, chopped
2 garlic cloves, finely chopped
1½-inch/4-cm piece fresh ginger, grated
1 tsp chili powder
1 tsp ground turmeric
1 tsp ground coriander
1 tsp garam masala
1 lb 2 oz/500 g ground beef
juice of ½ lemon
3 tbsp chopped fresh mint
chili sauce, to serve

Dough
2 cups all-purpose flour, plus extra for dusting
large pinch of salt
2 tbsp sunflower oil
about 5 tbsp lukewarm water

Spiced Beef & Pistachios

1. Preheat the oven to 375°F/190°C. Melt the butter in a pan. Add the onion, garlic, and chiles and cook over low heat, stirring occasionally, for 5 minutes. Add the ground beef, increase the heat to medium, and cook, stirring frequently and breaking it up with a wooden spoon, for 5–8 minutes, until evenly browned.

2. Remove the pan from the heat, stir in the pistachios, garam masala, tomatoes, breadcrumbs, and sour cream, and season to taste with salt and pepper. Mix well until thoroughly combined, then spoon the mixture into an ovenproof dish. Bake in the preheated oven for 35–45 minutes, until the top is lightly browned. Garnish with pistachios and serve immediately.

Serves 4

4 tbsp butter

1 Bermuda onion, chopped

2 garlic cloves, chopped

3 fresh green chiles, seeded and chopped

2 lb 4 oz/1 kg ground beef

2 tbsp coarsely chopped pistachios, plus extra to garnish

1½ tbsp garam masala

4 tomatoes, peeled and diced

4 tbsp fresh breadcrumbs

4 tbsp sour cream

salt and pepper

81

Pasta Shells with Aromatic Beef Sauce

1. Heat the oil in a skillet. Add the shallots and garlic and cook over low heat, stirring occasionally, for 5 minutes, until softened. Add the ground beef, increase the heat to medium, and cook, stirring frequently and breaking it up with a wooden spoon, for 8–10 minutes, until evenly browned. Drain off as much fat as possible.

2. Stir in the wine and simmer over low heat, stirring frequently, for 5 minutes. Add the mushrooms, cinnamon, allspice, parsley, torn basil, tomatoes, and ketchup, then season to taste with salt and pepper and mix well. Cover and simmer over very low heat, stirring occasionally, for 1 hour. If the mixture seems to be drying out, add a little water.

3. Meanwhile, bring a large pan of salted water to a boil. Add the pasta, return to a boil, and cook for 8–10 minutes, or until tender but still firm to the bite. Drain and toss with the beef sauce. Garnish with basil sprigs and serve immediately.

Serves 4

2 tbsp sunflower oil

4 shallots, finely chopped

1 garlic clove, finely chopped

1 lb/450 g ground beef

3 tbsp red wine

1⅔ cups chopped mushrooms

½ tsp ground cinnamon

½ tsp ground allspice

1 tbsp chopped fresh parsley

1 fresh basil sprig, leaves torn, plus extra sprigs to garnish

14 oz/400 g canned chopped tomatoes

2 tbsp ketchup

12 oz/350 g dried pasta shells

salt and pepper

82

Meatball Goulash

1. Tear the bread into pieces and put it into a small bowl. Add the milk and let soak for 5 minutes, then squeeze out the excess milk and put the bread into a large bowl. Add the ground beef, two-thirds of the garlic, the egg, orange rind, and 1 teaspoon of the dill, season to taste with salt and pepper, and mix well until thoroughly combined. Shape pieces of the mixture into small balls. Put the meatballs onto a plate, cover with plastic wrap, and chill in the refrigerator for 30 minutes.

2. Heat the oil in a large flameproof casserole. Add the onions, the remaining garlic, and the carrots and cook over low heat, stirring occasionally, for 5 minutes, until softened. Stir in the mushrooms and paprika and cook, stirring occasionally, for an additional 3 minutes. Pour in the stock and wine, add the caraway seeds and the remaining dill, and bring to a boil over medium heat, stirring constantly.

3. Add the meatballs to the casserole and bring back to a boil, then reduce the heat, cover, and simmer for 1 hour. Add the potatoes, re-cover the pan, and simmer for 20–25 minutes, until tender.

4. Mix the cornstarch to a paste with the water in a small bowl and add to the casserole with the sour cream. Cook, stirring constantly, for 2–3 minutes, until thickened, but do not let boil. Garnish with paprika and parsley and serve immediately.

Serves 4

4 slices rye bread, crusts removed

3 tbsp milk

2 lb 4 oz/1 kg ground beef

3 garlic cloves, finely chopped

1 egg, lightly beaten

1 tsp grated orange rind

1½ tsp dried dill

3 tbsp sunflower oil

2 onions, finely chopped

2 carrots, sliced

1⅔ cups thinly sliced mushrooms

1½ tbsp paprika, plus extra to garnish

1½ cups beef stock

½ cup red wine

1 tsp caraway seeds

4 potatoes, cut into chunks

2 tsp cornstarch

1 tbsp water

1¼ cups sour cream

salt and pepper

chopped fresh parsley, to garnish

Special

83

Chinese Soup with Meatballs

1. Put the mushrooms into a bowl and pour in warm water to cover. Let soak for 15 minutes, then drain and squeeze dry. Discard the stalks and thinly slice the caps.

2. Mix together the ground beef, onion, garlic, cornstarch, and egg in a bowl until thoroughly combined. Shape the mixture into small balls, drop them into a bowl of ice water, and let stand for 15 minutes.

3. Pour the stock into a large pan and bring to a boil. Drain the meatballs well, add to the pan, and bring back to a boil. Reduce the heat and simmer for 10 minutes. Add the mushrooms, watercress, scallions, and soy sauce to taste and simmer for an additional 2 minutes. Serve immediately.

Serves 4–6

5 dried Chinese mushrooms

12 oz/350 g ground beef

1 onion, finely chopped

1 garlic clove, finely chopped

1 tbsp cornstarch

1 egg, lightly beaten

3¾ cups beef stock

½ cup watercress, stalks removed

3 scallions, finely chopped

1–1½ tbsp soy sauce

84

Beef Soup with Ginger & Lemongrass

1. Put the noodles into a bowl, pour in hot water to cover, and let soak for 15–20 minutes, until soft. Drain and cut them into 2-inch/5-cm lengths.

2. Put the ground beef, shallots, and 1 tablespoon of the fish sauce into a large bowl, season to taste with pepper, and mix well. Cover with plastic wrap and chill in the refrigerator until required.

3. Heat half the oil in a large pan. Add the rice and ginger and cook over low heat, stirring constantly, for 1 minute. Pour in the water, increase the heat to medium, and bring to a boil. Partially cover the pan, reduce the heat, and simmer for 20 minutes, until tender. Stir in the sugar and the remaining fish sauce and season to taste with salt.

4. Heat the remaining oil in a small skillet. Add the garlic and lemongrass and cook over low–medium heat, stirring constantly, for 1 minute, then stir into the pan with the noodles and the ground beef mixture. Bring back to a boil, stirring constantly and breaking up the meat with a wooden spoon. Pour into warmed soup bowls and sprinkle with the peanuts, scallions, and cilantro. Serve immediately.

Serves 6

½ oz/15 g dried cellophane noodles

8 oz/225 g ground beef (preferably freshly ground steak)

2 shallots, finely chopped

4 tbsp Thai fish sauce

2 tbsp peanut oil

scant ½ cup long-grain rice

1 tsp grated fresh ginger

6¾ cups water

1 tbsp brown sugar

2 garlic cloves, very finely chopped

1 tbsp very finely chopped lemongrass

2 tbsp crushed unsalted roasted peanuts

2 scallions, thinly sliced

1 tbsp chopped fresh cilantro

salt and pepper

85

Beef & Pine Nut Triangles

1. Heat the oil in a large skillet. Add the onion and garlic and cook over low heat, stirring occasionally, for 5 minutes, until softened. Stir in the coriander and cumin and cook, stirring occasionally, for an additional 3 minutes. Add the ground beef, half the mint, and the pine nuts, increase the heat to medium, and cook, stirring and breaking up the meat with a wooden spoon, for 8–10 minutes, until evenly browned. Season to taste with salt and remove the skillet from the heat.

2. Meanwhile, cook the potatoes in a pan of salted boiling water for 15–20 minutes, until tender but not falling apart. Drain the potatoes, put into a bowl, and mash well, then stir in the cheese until melted. Stir in the ground beef mixture.

3. Preheat the oven to 400°F/200°C. Brush 2 baking sheets with a little of the melted butter. Brush 1 sheet of dough with melted butter, put a second sheet on top, and brush with more melted butter. Cut the double layer lengthwise into 3 strips. Put a heaping tablespoon of the filling near the end of a strip, then fold over the corner to form a triangle. Continue to fold over in triangles to make a neat package, then put it on a prepared baking sheet. Make 14 more triangles in the same way. Brush the triangles with the remaining melted butter and bake in the preheated oven for 8–10 minutes, until golden brown.

4. Meanwhile, stir the remaining mint into the tomato sauce and reheat gently. Serve the filo triangles with the tomato-and-mint sauce.

Makes 15

1 tbsp olive oil

* 1 small onion, chopped

* 2 garlic cloves, finely chopped

1 tsp ground coriander

1 tsp ground cumin

* 10½ oz/300 g ground beef

4 tbsp chopped fresh mint

2 tbsp pine nuts

2 potatoes, cut into chunks

½ cup grated Kefalotiri or cheddar cheese

½ cup melted butter

10 sheets filo dough

1 quantity Tomato Sauce (see page 58)

* salt

Russian Beef & Onion Pastries

1. For the dough, sift the flour and salt into a bowl. Add the cream cheese and butter, then rub in with your fingertips until the mixture resembles breadcrumbs. Add 1 tablespoon of the water and mix in, then add 1 tablespoon of the cream and mix in. Repeat twice more. Knead gently, adding a little more water if necessary, then shape into a ball, cover, and chill in the refrigerator for 30 minutes.

2. Meanwhile, melt the butter in a pan. Add the onion and cook over low heat, stirring occasionally, for 5 minutes, until softened. Add the ground beef, increase the heat to medium, and cook, stirring frequently and breaking it up with a wooden spoon, for 8–10 minutes, until evenly browned. Remove the pan from the heat, stir in the rice, sour cream, Worcestershire sauce, caraway seeds, and hard-cooked egg, and season to taste with salt and pepper.

3. Preheat the oven to 400°F/200°C. Grease 2 baking sheets. Roll out the dough on a lightly floured surface to a thickness of ⅛ inch/3 mm and stamp out circles with a 3¼-inch/8-cm plain cutter. Put a teaspoon of the ground beef mixture on 1 side of each dough circle, brush the edges with a little of the beaten egg, and fold over. Press the edges with a fork or your finger to seal. Transfer to the prepared baking sheets and brush with the remaining beaten egg. Bake in the preheated oven for 20 minutes, until golden brown. Serve immediately.

Makes 40–45

4 tbsp butter, plus extra for greasing
1 onion, finely chopped
8 oz/225 g ground beef
⅓ cup cooked rice
2 tbsp sour cream
1 tsp Worcestershire sauce
1 tsp caraway seeds
1 hard-cooked egg, chopped
1 egg, beaten with 1 tsp water
salt and pepper

Dough
3 cups all-purpose flour, plus extra for dusting
pinch of salt
¼ cup cream cheese
½ cup butter
about 3 tbsp water
3 tbsp heavy cream

87

Beef & Wild Rice

1. Preheat the oven to 350°F/180°C. Drain the rice and put it into a bowl. Add the ground beef, onions, garlic, carrots, mustard, and eggs and season to taste with salt and pepper. Mix well with your hands until thoroughly combined.

2. Spoon the mixture into a 9 x 5 x 3-inch/23 x 13 x 8-cm loaf pan and smooth the surface. Bake in the preheated oven for 1½ hours, until the juices run clear when a skewer is inserted into the center.

3. Remove the pan from the oven and pour off any fat. Run a round-bladed knife around the edge of the pan and turn out onto a warmed serving plate. Garnish with sage leaves and serve immediately with the tomato sauce.

Serves 6

generous ½ cup wild rice, rinsed and soaked overnight

1 lb 2 oz/500 g ground beef

2 onions, finely chopped

2 garlic cloves, finely chopped

4 carrots, grated

1 tbsp Dijon mustard

2 eggs, lightly beaten

salt and pepper

fresh sage leaves, to garnish

1 quantity Tomato Sauce, to serve (see page 58)

Beef Pilaf

① Heat 3 tablespoons of the oil in a pan. Add two-thirds of the onions and two-thirds of the garlic and cook over low heat, stirring occasionally, for 5 minutes, until softened. Add the rice, ground cumin, turmeric, and coriander and cook, stirring constantly, for 1 minute. Pour in the stock and bring to a boil. Stir well, reduce the heat, cover, and simmer for 15–20 minutes, until the rice is tender and the liquid has been absorbed.

② Meanwhile, put the remaining onion, remaining garlic, the ground beef, mace, cumin seeds, and mint into a bowl. Season to taste with salt and pepper and mix well with your hands until thoroughly combined. Shape into walnut-size balls.

③ Heat the remaining oil in a skillet. Add the meatballs and cook over medium heat, turning occasionally, for 6–8 minutes, until evenly browned and cooked through. Remove from the skillet and drain on paper towels.

④ Remove the rice mixture from the heat and stir in the butter, then gently stir in the meatballs. Transfer to a warmed serving dish, garnish with cilantro sprigs, and serve immediately.

Serves 4–6

½ cup olive oil
3 onions, finely chopped
3 garlic cloves, finely chopped
4 cups long-grain rice
1 tsp ground cumin
1 tsp ground turmeric
1 tsp ground coriander
7½ cups beef stock
1 lb 5 oz/600 g ground beef
pinch of ground mace
1 tsp cumin seeds
2 tbsp chopped fresh mint
½ cup butter
salt and pepper
fresh cilantro sprigs, to garnish

Puff Pastry Meat Loaf

① Preheat the oven to 350°F/180°C. Grease a 10 x 5 x 3-inch/ 25 x 13 x 7.5-cm loaf pan. Put the ground beef, breadcrumbs, onions, garlic, apples, mustard, and parsley into a bowl and mix well. Beat 1 of the eggs with the stock and add to the bowl. Season to taste with salt and pepper and mix until thoroughly combined.

② Spoon the mixture into the prepared pan. Stand the loaf pan in a roasting pan and pour in water to come about halfway up the sides. Bake in the preheated oven for 45 minutes. Remove from the oven and remove the loaf pan from the roasting pan. Cover with wax paper, weigh down lightly with small cans, and let cool completely. Remove the cans and paper and turn out when cold.

③ Preheat the oven to 425°F/220°C. Roll out the dough on a lightly floured surface to a thickness of ⅛–¼ inch/3–5 mm. Put the meat loaf in the center of the dough, brush the edges of the dough with water, and fold over to enclose the meat loaf completely, trimming off any excess dough. Put the package on a baking sheet, seam-side down. Roll out the dough trimmings and make decorations. Brush with water and arrange on top of the package. Lightly beat the remaining egg and brush it over the package, then make 2–3 slits in the dough.

④ Bake in the preheated oven for 35 minutes, until the pastry is puffed up and golden brown. If serving cold, remove from the oven and let cool. If serving hot, reduce the oven temperature to 350°F/180°C and bake for an additional 10 minutes.

Serves 4

butter, for greasing
* 12 oz/350 g ground beef
1 cup fresh breadcrumbs
* 2 onions, finely chopped
* 1 garlic clove, finely chopped
2 tart apples, peeled, cored, and finely chopped
1 tbsp Dijon mustard
2 tbsp chopped fresh parsley
2 eggs
4 tbsp beef stock
10½ oz/300 g store-bought puff pastry, thawed if frozen
all-purpose flour, for dusting
* salt and pepper

90

Italian Croquettes

1. Cook the rice in a large pan of salted boiling water for 15–20 minutes, until tender. Drain, rinse with boiling water, and return to the pan. Stir in half the butter, the Parmesan, and parsley. Spread out on a baking sheet and let cool.

2. Meanwhile, heat the remaining butter with the olive oil in a pan. Add the shallot and garlic and cook over low heat, stirring occasionally, for 5 minutes, until softened. Add the ground beef, increase the heat to medium, and cook, stirring frequently and breaking it up with a wooden spoon, for 5–8 minutes, until evenly browned. Stir in the wine and cook for 5 minutes. Reduce the heat and stir in the tomato paste, then cover and simmer for 15 minutes. Season to taste with salt and pepper and remove from the heat.

3. When the rice mixture is cold, shape it into balls about the size of a large egg and make a small hollow in each. Put a spoonful of ground beef mixture and a cube of cheese in each hollow, then reshape to enclose the filling completely.

4. Lightly beat the eggs in a shallow dish and spread out the flour in a separate shallow dish. Dip the croquettes first in the egg and then in the flour to coat. Heat enough sunflower oil for deep-frying in a deep-fryer to 350–375°F/180–190°C, or until a cube of bread browns in 30 seconds. Add the croquettes, in batches, and fry until golden brown all over. Drain on paper towels and serve immediately.

Serves 4

1½ cups long-grain rice
4 tbsp butter
2 tbsp grated Parmesan cheese
1 tbsp chopped fresh parsley
1 tbsp olive oil
1 shallot, finely chopped
1 garlic clove, finely chopped
4 oz/115 g ground beef
scant ½ cup dry white wine
2 tbsp tomato paste
1 cup cubed mozzarella cheese
2 eggs
½ cup all-purpose flour
sunflower oil, for deep-frying
salt and pepper

French Beef Patties in Red Wine

1. Melt 2 tablespoons of the butter in a skillet. Add the onions and garlic and cook over low heat, stirring occasionally, for 5 minutes, until softened. Transfer the mixture to a bowl, add the ground beef, oregano, parsley, and egg, and season to taste with salt and pepper. Mix well with your hands until thoroughly combined.

2. Shape the mixture into 4 patties, each about ¾ inch/2 cm thick. Dust with the flour, gently shaking off the excess.

3. Melt half the remaining butter with the oil in a skillet. Add the patties and cook for 3–4 minutes on each side, until cooked to your liking. Using a spatula, transfer the patties to a serving dish and keep warm.

4. Pour off the fat from the skillet, then add the wine and bring to a boil over medium–high heat. Boil until it is reduced by about half. Meanwhile, dice the remaining butter. Remove the skillet from the heat and whisk in the butter, 1 piece at a time, making sure each piece has been incorporated before adding the next. Pour the sauce over the patties, garnish with parsley, and serve immediately.

Serves 4

6 tbsp butter
* 2 red onions, finely chopped
* 1 garlic clove, finely chopped
* 1 lb 7 oz/650 g ground beef
½ tsp dried oregano
1 tbsp chopped fresh parsley, plus extra to garnish
1 egg, lightly beaten
½ cup all-purpose flour
1 tbsp olive oil
⅔ cup red wine
* salt and pepper

Beef & Pumpkin Baked with Rice

1. Put the onion, ground beef, mint, and cinnamon into a bowl and mix well until thoroughly combined. Season to taste with salt and pepper. Divide the mixture into 8 equal-size portions and shape into small patties.

2. Melt 4 tablespoons of the butter in a skillet. Add the patties, in batches if necessary, and cook for 3–4 minutes on each side, until lightly browned. Remove with a spatula.

3. Preheat the oven to 375°F/190°C. Grease a large casserole. Cook the rice in a large pan of salted boiling water for 15–20 minutes, until tender. Drain well and rinse with boiling water.

4. Spoon half the rice into the prepared casserole. Melt the remaining butter and pour half of it over the rice. Put the beef patties on top and cover with the remaining rice. Spread the pumpkin cubes over the top, sprinkle with the sugar, and pour the remaining melted butter over them. Cover and bake in the preheated oven for 25–30 minutes, until the pumpkin is tender. Serve immediately.

Serves 4

- 1 onion, finely chopped
- 1 lb 2 oz/500 g ground beef
- 1 tbsp finely chopped fresh mint
- ½ tsp ground cinnamon
- ¾ cup butter, plus extra for greasing
- generous 1 cup long-grain rice
- 1 lb 2 oz/500 g pumpkin or squash, peeled, seeded, and cut into cubes
- 2 tbsp brown sugar
- salt and pepper

93

Lemon Beef in Walnut Sauce

1. Tear the bread into pieces, put it into a large bowl with the milk, and let soak for 5 minutes. Add the ground beef, garlic, lemon rind, and egg, season to taste with salt and pepper, and mix well until thoroughly combined. Using your hands, shape pieces of the mixture into walnut-size meatballs.

2. Melt 4 tablespoons of the butter in a skillet. Add the meatballs, in batches, and cook over medium heat, turning frequently, for 5 minutes, until browned all over. Remove with a slotted spoon.

3. Melt the remaining butter in a large pan. Add the onions and cook over low heat, stirring occasionally, for 5 minutes, until softened. Add the walnuts and cook, stirring frequently, for an additional 5 minutes. Pour in the water and bring to a boil. Add the pomegranate juice, lemon juice, and sugar and season to taste with salt and pepper. Reduce the heat and simmer, stirring frequently, for 30 minutes.

4. Add the meatballs to the pan and simmer very gently for 1½ hours, until almost all the liquid has been absorbed. Transfer to a warmed serving dish, garnish with strips of lemon zest, and serve immediately.

Serves 4

1 slice white bread, crusts removed
2 tbsp milk
1 lb 2 oz/500 g ground beef
1 garlic clove, finely chopped
1 tbsp finely grated lemon rind
1 egg, lightly beaten
6 tbsp butter
3 onions, finely chopped
1¼ cups finely chopped walnuts
2½ cups water
5 tbsp pomegranate juice
1 tbsp lemon juice
1½ tbsp sugar
salt and pepper
strips of lemon zest, to garnish

Beef with Bell Pepper, Fruit & Nuts

1. Heat the oil in a large skillet. Add the onions, garlic, celery, and bell pepper and cook over low heat, stirring occasionally, for 5 minutes. Add the ground beef, increase the heat to medium, and cook, stirring frequently and breaking it up with a wooden spoon, for 8–10 minutes, until evenly browned.

2. Add the tomatoes, cannellini beans, tomato paste, chili powder, nutmeg, apples, apricots, slivered almonds, and green beans. Season to taste with salt and pepper. Reduce the heat, cover, and simmer for 30 minutes, then remove the lid and simmer for an additional 10 minutes. Garnish with slivered almonds and serve immediately.

Serves 4

3 tbsp sunflower oil

2 onions, finely chopped

2 garlic cloves, finely chopped

2 celery stalks, chopped

1 red bell pepper, seeded and chopped

2 lb 4 oz/1 kg ground beef

14 oz/400 g canned chopped tomatoes

14 oz/400 g canned cannellini beans, drained and rinsed

6 tbsp tomato paste

1 tsp chili powder

½ tsp ground nutmeg

2 tart green apples, cored and chopped

¼ cup chopped dried apricots

2 tbsp slivered almonds, plus extra to garnish

¾ cup frozen green beans, thawed

salt and pepper

Stuffed Beef Rolls

1. Preheat the oven to 350°F/180°C. Put the ground beef, shallot, butter, breadcrumbs, lemon rind, and olives into a bowl and mix well. Add the egg, season to taste with salt and pepper, and mix until thoroughly combined. Divide the mixture among the beef slices, then roll up and tie with kitchen string.

2. Heat the oil in a flameproof casserole. Add the beef rolls, in batches, and cook over low–medium heat, turning occasionally, until browned all over. Remove with a slotted spoon and set aside.

3. Add the onions, garlic, and carrots to the casserole and cook over low heat, stirring occasionally, for 5 minutes. Add the stock, tomatoes, and bay leaf and bring to a boil. Remove the casserole from the heat and return the beef rolls to it, then cover and cook in the preheated oven for 1½ hours.

4. Remove the casserole from the oven and lift out the beef rolls. Carefully remove and discard the string and put the rolls on a warmed serving plate. Strain the cooking liquid into a pitcher, pressing down on the vegetables with the back of a spoon. Taste and adjust the seasoning, adding salt and pepper if needed, then pour the sauce over the beef rolls. Sprinkle with the parsley and serve immediately.

Serves 4

6 oz/175 g ground beef
1 shallot, finely chopped
2 tbsp butter
½ cup fresh breadcrumbs
grated rind of 1 lemon
6 green olives, pitted and chopped
1 egg, lightly beaten
8 slices top round steak, about ¼ inch/5 mm thick
2 tbsp olive oil
2 onions, finely chopped
1 garlic clove, finely chopped
2 carrots, finely chopped
1¼ cups beef stock
2 tomatoes, peeled, seeded, and sliced
1 bay leaf
3 tbsp finely chopped fresh parsley
salt and pepper

96

Ground Beef Stroganoff

1. Heat 2 tablespoons of the oil in a large skillet. Add the onion and garlic and cook over low heat, stirring occasionally, for 5 minutes, until softened. Add the mushrooms and cook, stirring frequently, for an additional 5 minutes. Using a slotted spoon, transfer the vegetables to a plate.

2. Add the remaining oil to the skillet, then add the ground beef and cook over medium heat, stirring frequently and breaking it up with a wooden spoon, for 5–8 minutes, until evenly browned. Drain off as much fat as possible.

3. Reduce the heat to low, return the vegetables to the skillet, and stir in the brandy. Cook, stirring occasionally, for 4–5 minutes, until the alcohol has evaporated. Stir in the stock, season to taste with salt and pepper, and simmer gently, stirring frequently, for 15 minutes.

4. Stir in the sour cream and parsley and cook for an additional minute. Garnish with parsley and serve immediately.

Serves 4

3 tbsp sunflower oil
* 1 onion, chopped
* 2 garlic cloves, finely chopped
4⅓ cups sliced mushrooms
* 1 lb 2 oz/500 g ground beef
2 tbsp brandy
⅔ cup beef stock
⅔ cup sour cream
2 tbsp chopped fresh parsley, plus extra to garnish
* salt and pepper

Beef Roulade

1. Preheat the oven to 375°F/190°C. Heat the oil in a pan. Add the onion and garlic and cook over low heat, stirring occasionally, for 5 minutes, until softened. Add the ground beef, increase the heat to medium, and cook, stirring frequently and breaking it up with a wooden spoon, for 8–10 minutes, until evenly browned. Remove from the heat and drain off as much fat as possible. Stir in the herbs, season to taste with salt and pepper, and let cool.

2. Put the beef slices, slightly overlapping, on a sheet of plastic wrap. Cover with a second sheet of plastic wrap and beat with a meat mallet until thin and joined together. Carefully transfer the beaten beef to a board and gently remove the plastic wrap. Spread the beef with the cream cheese.

3. Spoon the ground beef mixture evenly over the top and roll up. Tie with kitchen string. Put the roulade in a roasting pan and brush with the barbecue sauce. Cook in the preheated oven for 1 1¼ hours, until tender

4. Remove the pan from the oven and transfer the roulade to a board. Remove and discard the string, cut the roulade into slices, and serve immediately.

Serves 4

1 tbsp olive oil
1 small onion, finely chopped
1 garlic clove, finely chopped
4 oz/115 g ground beef
1 tbsp chopped fresh parsley
1 tbsp snipped fresh chives
8 slices top round steak, about ⅜ inch/8 mm thick
1 cup cream cheese with garlic and herbs
2 tbsp barbecue sauce
salt and pepper

Eggplant Rolls

1. Heat 2 tablespoons of the oil in a skillet. Add the onion and garlic and cook over low heat, stirring occasionally, for 5 minutes, until softened. Add the ground beef, increase the heat to medium, and cook, stirring frequently and breaking it up with a wooden spoon, for 8–10 minutes, until evenly browned. Pour off as much fat as possible.

2. Return the pan to the heat and add the tomatoes. Season to taste with salt and pepper and simmer gently for 15–20 minutes, until thickened. Remove from the heat and let cool. Stir the egg, cheese, and nutmeg into the béchamel sauce, then stir the sauce into the ground beef mixture.

3. Preheat the oven to 350°F/180°C. Heat half the remaining oil in a skillet. Add the eggplant slices, in batches, and cook for a few minutes on both sides, until golden brown. Drain on paper towels.

4. Brush a baking sheet with oil. Stack 3 sheets of dough, brushing each with some of the remaining oil. Put half the eggplant slices along 1 long edge, leaving 2 inches/5 cm at each end. Top them with half the ground beef mixture, spreading it evenly, and roll up the dough. Repeat to make a second roll.

5. Put the rolls onto the prepared baking sheet and brush with oil. Bake in the preheated oven for 35–40 minutes, until golden brown. Serve immediately.

Serves 4

scant ½ cup olive oil, plus extra for brushing

* 1 onion, grated
* 1 garlic clove, very finely chopped
* 8 oz/225 g ground beef

2 tomatoes, peeled, seeded, and chopped

1 egg, lightly beaten

¾ cup grated Gruyère cheese

pinch of ground nutmeg

½ cup Béchamel Sauce (see page 70)

3 eggplants, peeled and cut into ¼ inch/5 mm thick slices

6 sheets filo dough

* salt and pepper

99

Glazed Beef

① Brush a 6¼-cup heatproof bowl with oil. Cut out a circle of wax paper and a circle of aluminum foil 4 inches/10 cm larger than the diameter of the bowl. Holding them together, make a 1-inch/2.5-cm pleat in the center.

② Put the ground beef, ham, shallots, breadcrumbs, ketchup, and herbs into a large bowl. Season to taste with salt and pepper. Add the eggs and mix until thoroughly combined. Spoon the mixture into the prepared bowl, cover with the cutout circles, foil-side uppermost, and tie with kitchen string.

③ Put the bowl into a large pan and carefully pour in boiling water to come about halfway up the side. Cover and steam for 3 hours, adding extra boiling water as necessary. Remove the bowl from the pan. Remove and discard the coverings and pour off any excess fat. Invert the mold onto a serving plate and let cool, then chill in the refrigerator for 1 hour.

④ Pour the water into a small bowl, sprinkle the gelatin over the surface, and let soak for 5 minutes, until spongy. Pour the gelatin mixture into a pan and heat gently until the gelatin has dissolved. Add the stock and tomato paste, season to taste with salt and pepper, and heat gently, stirring until combined. Remove from the heat and let cool. When the gelatin mixture is cool, but not set, brush it all over the mold. Chill in the refrigerator until set.

Serves 4–6

sunflower oil, for brushing
✳ 1 lb 2 oz/500 g ground beef
1 lb 2 oz/500 g ham, very finely chopped
✳ 2 shallots, finely chopped
1 cup fresh breadcrumbs
1 tbsp ketchup
2 tsp chopped fresh thyme
1 tbsp chopped fresh parsley
2 eggs, lightly beaten
3 tbsp water
3½ tsp powdered gelatin
1¼ cups beef stock
1 tbsp tomato paste
✳ salt and pepper

100

Chinese Noodles with Beef & Shredded Vegetables

1. Cook the noodles in a large pan of salted boiling water according to the package directions, then drain and keep warm.

2. Heat a wok over medium heat, then add the peanut oil, swirl it around, and heat. Add the scallions, garlic, and ginger and stir-fry for 2 minutes. Add the ground beef and stir-fry, breaking it up with a wooden spoon, for 5 minutes, until evenly browned. Stir in the sesame oil, soy sauce, rice wine, and sugar and cook, stirring constantly, for an additional 3 minutes.

3. Mix the cornstarch to a paste with the water in a small bowl and add to the wok. Simmer, stirring constantly, until the sauce has thickened and become glossy.

4. Divide the noodles among individual bowls and top with the ground beef mixture and shredded vegetables. Serve immediately.

Serves 4

1 lb 2 oz/500 g dried egg noodles

3 tbsp peanut oil

3 scallions, thinly sliced

2 garlic cloves, finely chopped

½-inch/1-cm piece fresh ginger, finely chopped

12 oz/350 g ground beef

1 tbsp sesame oil

5 tbsp soy sauce

2 tbsp Chinese rice wine or dry sherry

1 tbsp sugar

1 tbsp cornstarch

4 tbsp water

salt

To serve

2 cups blanched fresh bean sprouts

1¼ cups blanched shredded Chinese cabbage

¾ cup blanched shredded carrots

1 cup shredded cucumber

1 cup shredded radishes

apples
  Beef with Bell Pepper, Fruit & Nuts 209
  Puff Pastry Meat Loaf 198
apricots: Beef with Bell Pepper, Fruit & Nuts 209
avocados
  Fiery Beef Tacos 150
  Taco Soup 142

bacon
  Bacon Burgers 19
  Béchamel Lasagna 70
  Bolognese Soufflé 126
  Meat Loaf 63
  Spaghetti Bolognese 64
  Stuffed Baked Potatoes 81
Baked Beef & Potato Layers 107
Basic Ground Beef Mix 10
Battered Beef 44
bean sprouts
  Beef & Noodles 26
  Chinese Noodles with Beef & Shredded Vegetables 221
beans
  Beef & Vegetable Gratin 137
  Beef 'n' Beans 87
  Beef with Bell Pepper, Fruit & Nuts 209
  Burritos 153
  see also kidney beans; refried beans
beets: Hamburgers with Beet 128
bell peppers
  Beef & Noodles 26
  Beef & Vegetable Gratin 137
  Beef with Bell Pepper, Fruit & Nuts 209
  Beef with Scrambled Eggs 22
  Burritos 153
  Empanadas 154
  Ground Beef Casserole 102
  Ground Beef Hash 88
  Ground Beef Pizza 82
  Mexican Beef Stew 159
  Quick Curry 31
  Sloppy Joes 72
  Spaghetti & Meatballs 69
  Stir-Fried Beef 25
  Stuffed Bell Peppers 76
  see also pimientos
Bolognese Soufflé 126
Braised Hamburgers 104
breadcrumbs
  Bacon Burgers 19
  Beef & Cheese Roll 131
  Beef & Potato Rissoles 49
  Chili Burgers 144
  Glazed Beef 218
  Indian Kabobs 171
  Indian Potato Cakes 174
  Lemon Beef in Walnut Sauce 206
  Meat Loaf 63
  Meatball Goulash 183
  Meatballs 58
  Salisbury Steak 93
  Savory Croquettes 46
  Spaghetti & Meatballs 69
  Spiced Beef & Pistachios 178
  Spicy Ground Beef Casserole 165
  Stuffed Beef Rolls 210
  Stuffed Onions 52
  Swedish Meatballs 60
broccoli: Stir-Fried Beef 25
burgers
  Bacon Burgers 19
  Braised Hamburgers 104
  Cheese-Stuffed Hamburgers 75
  Chili Burgers 144
  Hamburgers with Beet 128
  Homemade Hamburgers 16
Burritos 153

Cabbage Rolls 50
capers
  Beef Tamale 160
  Hamburgers with Beet 128
carrots
  Béchamel Lasagna 70
  Beef & Noodles 26
  Beef & Tomato Soup 14
  Beef & Vegetable Gratin 137
  Beef & Wild Rice 194
  Beef with Garlic Potatoes 101
  Beef-Filled Crêpes 116

Chinese Noodles with Beef & Shredded Vegetables 221
Ground Beef & Mashed Vegetables 78
Ground Beef with Potato Topping 98
Lasagna 40
Meatball Goulash 183
Simple Savory Beef 90
Spaghetti Bolognese 64
Stir-Fried Beef 25
Stuffed Beef Rolls 210
celery
  Béchamel Lasagna 70
  Beef with Bell Pepper, Fruit & Nuts 209
  Braised Hamburgers 104
  One-Pot Pasta 38
  Spaghetti Bolognese 64
  Stuffed Baked Potatoes 81
cheese
  Baked Beef & Potato Layers 107
  Beef & Cheese Cobbler 120
  Beef & Pine Nut Triangles 191
  Beef & Vegetable Gratin 137
  Beef Potpie 119
  Burritos 153
  Cheese-Stuffed Hamburgers 75
  Eggplant Rolls 216
  Enchiladas 147
  Fiery Beef Tacos 150
  Greek Baked Pasta 125
  Ground Beef Casserole 102
  Ground Beef with Potato Topping 98
  Lasagna 40
  Meaty Macaroni & Cheese 66
  Meaty Muffins 55
  Nachos 156
  Taco Soup 142
  Tamale Pie 96
  Tex-Mex Pizza 34
  see also cream cheese; feta cheese; mozzarella cheese;
    Parmesan cheese
chicken livers: Spaghetti Bolognese 64
chiles/chili powder
  Beef & Noodles 26
  Beef & Tomato Soup 14
  Beef Samosas 177
  Beef Tamale 160
  Beef with Bell Pepper, Fruit & Nuts 209
  Burritos 153
  Chili Burgers 144
  Chili con Carne 148
  Curry Puffs 168
  Empanadas 154
  Enchiladas 147
  Fiery Beef Tacos 150
  Indian Kabobs 171
  Indian Potato Cakes 174
  Mexican Beef Stew 159
  Nachos 156
  Quick Curry 31
  Spiced Beef & Pistachios 178
  Spicy Beef & Sweet Potatoes 162
  Stuffed Bell Peppers 76
  Taco Soup 142
  Tamale Pie 96
  Tex-Mex Pizza 34
  Thai Beef Omelet 32
Chili con Carne 148
Chinese cabbage: Chinese Noodles with Beef & Shredded
    Vegetables 221
Chinese Noodles with Beef & Shredded Vegetables 221
Chinese Soup with Meatballs 186
chives
  Beef & Potato Rissoles 49
  Beef Roulade 215
  Meal-in-a-Bowl Beef & Herb Soup 132
cilantro
  Beef Curry 172
  Beef in Pita Pockets 84
  Beef Keftas 20
  Beef Soup with Ginger & Lemongrass 188
  Burritos 153
  Chili Burgers 144
  Ground Beef Pizza 82
  Indian Kabobs 171
  Indian Potato Cakes 174
  Meal-in-a-Bowl Beef & Herb Soup 132
  Mexican Beef Stew 159
  Quick Curry 31
  Thai Beef Omelet 32

corn
  Beef & Vegetable Gratin 137
  Beef Tamale 160
  Meaty Macaroni & Cheese 66
  Meaty Muffins 55
  Mexican Beef Stew 159
  Stir-Fried Beef 25
  Tamale Pie 96
cornmeal: Tamale Pie 96
cream
  Beef & Spinach Cannelloni 138
  Dutch Crêpe Cake 134
  Enchiladas 147
  Ground Beef & Mashed Vegetables 78
  Stuffed Bell Peppers 76
  Swedish Meatballs 60
  see also sour cream
cream cheese
  Beef 'n' Beans 87
  Beef Roulade 215
  Russian Beef & Onion Pastries 192
  Stuffed Bell Peppers 76
crêpes
  Beef-Filled Crêpes 116
  Dutch Crêpe Cake 134
Crispy Beef Fritters 37
croquettes
  Italian Croquettes 200
  Savory Croquettes 46
curry
  Beef Curry 172
  Beef Samosas 177
  Curry Puffs 168
  Indonesian Beef Parcels 166
  Quick Curry 31
  Spiced Beef & Pistachios 178
  Spicy Ground Beef Casserole 165

dumplings: Fried Beef Dumplings 114
Dutch Crêpe Cake 134

eggplants
  Eggplant Rolls 216
  Greek Baked Pasta 125
  Ground Beef Casserole 102
  Layered Beef & Feta 108
eggs
  Battered Beef 44
  Beef & Cheese Roll 131
  Beef & Potato Rissoles 49
  Beef & Vegetable Gratin 137
  Beef & Wild Rice 194
  Beef Fried Rice 28
  Beef Tamale 160
  Beef with Scrambled Eggs 22
  Bolognese Soufflé 126
  Crispy Beef Fritters 37
  Glazed Beef 218
  Greek Baked Pasta 125
  Ground Beef Hash 88
  Hamburgers with Beet 128
  Indian Potato Cakes 174
  Indonesian Beef Parcels 166
  Italian Croquettes 200
  Layered Beef & Feta 108
  Meat Loaf 63
  Meaty Muffins 55
  Puff Pastry Meat Loaf 198
  Russian Beef & Onion Pastries 192
  Savory Croquettes 46
  Spicy Ground Beef Casserole 165
  Stuffed Onions 52
  Thai Beef Omelet 32
Empanadas 154
Enchiladas 147

feta cheese
  Layered Beef & Feta 108
  Stuffed Baked Potatoes 81
Fiery Beef Tacos 150
French Beef Patties in Red Wine 203
French Meat Tart 122
Fried Beef Dumplings 114

garlic
  Bacon Burgers 19
  Baked Beef & Potato Layers 107
  Basic Ground Beef Mix 10
  Battered Beef 44

Béchamel Lasagna 70
Beef & Pine Nut Triangles 191
Beef & Spinach Cannelloni 138
Beef & Tomato Soup 14
Beef & Vegetable Gratin 137
Beef & Wild Rice 194
Beef Curry 172
Beef Fried Rice 28
Beef in Pita Pockets 84
Beef Keftas 20
Beef Pilaf 197
Beef Potpie 119
Beef Roulade 215
Beef Samosas 177
Beef Soup with Ginger & Lemongrass 188
Beef with Bell Pepper, Fruit & Nuts 209
Beef with Garlic Potatoes 101
Beef with Pimientos 110
Beef with Scrambled Eggs 22
Beefy Baked Potatoes 43
Bolognese Soufflé 126
Braised Hamburgers 104
Burritos 153
Cabbage Rolls 50
Cheese-Stuffed Hamburgers 75
Chili con Carne 148
Chinese Noodles with Beef & Shredded Vegetables 221
Chinese Soup with Meatballs 186
Curry Puffs 168
Eggplant Rolls 216
Empanadas 154
Enchiladas 147
Fiery Beef Tacos 150
French Beef Patties in Red Wine 203
French Meat Tart 122
Greek Baked Pasta 125
Ground Beef Pizza 82
Ground Beef Stroganoff 212
Ground Beef with Potato Topping 98
Indian Kabobs 171
Indian Potato Cakes 174
Indonesian Beef Parcels 166
Italian Croquettes 200
Lasagna 40
Layered Beef & Feta 108
Lemon Beef in Walnut Sauce 206
Meal-in-a-Bowl Beef & Herb Soup 132
Meat Loaf 63
Meatball Goulash 183
Meatballs 58
Meaty Macaroni & Cheese 66
Mexican Beef Stew 159
Nachos 156
One-Pot Pasta 38
Pasta Shells with Aromatic Beef Sauce 180
Puff Pastry Meat Loaf 198
Quick Curry 31
Savory Croquettes 46
Sloppy Joes 72
Spaghetti & Meatballs 69
Spaghetti Bolognese 64
Spiced Beef & Pistachios 178
Spicy Beef & Sweet Potatoes 162
Spicy Ground Beef Casserole 165
Stir-Fried Beef 25
Stuffed Baked Potatoes 81
Stuffed Beef Rolls 210
Stuffed Bell Peppers 76
Stuffed Onions 52
Tex-Mex Pizza 34
Thai Beef Omelet 32
ginger
    Beef & Noodles 26
    Beef Curry 172
    Beef Samosas 177
    Beef Soup with Ginger & Lemongrass 188
    Chinese Noodles with Beef & Shredded Vegetables 221
    Curry Puffs 168
    Indian Kabobs 171
    Indian Potato Cakes 174
    Stir-Fried Beef 25
Glazed Beef 218
Greek Baked Pasta 125
green beans: Beef with Bell Pepper, Fruit & Nuts 209

ham
    Beef Tamale 160
    Glazed Beef 218

horseradish
    Cheese-Stuffed Hamburgers 75
    Salisbury Steak 93

Indian Kabobs 171
Indian Potato Cakes 174
Indonesian Beef Parcels 166
Italian Croquettes 200

kidney beans
    Chili con Carne 148
    Mexican Beef Stew 159
    Taco Soup 142

lasagna
    Béchamel Lasagna 70
    Lasagna 40
Layered Beef & Feta 108
Lemon Beef in Walnut Sauce 206

Meal-in-a-Bowl Beef & Herb Soup 132
Meat Loaf 63
Meatballs 58
    Chinese Soup with Meatballs 186
    Meatball Goulash 183
    Meatballs 58
    Spaghetti & Meatballs 69
    Swedish Meatballs 60
Meaty Macaroni & Cheese 66
Meaty Muffins 55
Mexican Beef Stew 159
mint
    Beef & Pine Nut Triangles 191
    Beef & Pumpkin Baked with Rice 204
    Beef Keftas 20
    Beef Pilaf 197
    Beef Samosas 177
    Indian Potato Cakes 174
    Meal-in-a-Bowl Beef & Herb Soup 132
mozzarella cheese
    Beef & Cheese Roll 131
    Ground Beef Pizza 82
    Italian Croquettes 200
    Lasagna 40
mushrooms
    Beef Potpie 119
    Chinese Soup with Meatballs 186
    Dutch Crêpe Cake 134
    Ground Beef Stroganoff 212
    Ground Beef with Potato Topping 98
    Meat Loaf 63
    Meatball Goulash 183
    One-Pot Pasta 38
    Pasta Shells with Aromatic Beef Sauce 180
    Salisbury Steak 93
    Spaghetti Bolognese 64
mustard
    Beef & Cheese Roll 131
    Beef & Wild Rice 194
    Beef 'n' Beans 87
    Meat Loaf 63
    Meaty Macaroni & Cheese 66
    Puff Pastry Meat Loaf 198
    Salisbury Steak 93
    Simple Savory Beef 90
    Sloppy Joes 72

Nachos 156
noodles
    Beef & Noodles 26
    Beef Soup with Ginger & Lemongrass 188
    Chinese Noodles with Beef & Shredded Vegetables 221
nuts
    Beef Soup with Ginger & Lemongrass 188
    Beef with Bell Pepper, Fruit & Nuts 209
    Lemon Beef in Walnut Sauce 206
    Spiced Beef & Pistachios 178
    Spicy Ground Beef Casserole 165

oats
    Fried Beef Dumplings 114
    Ground Beef & Mashed Vegetables 78
olives
    Beef Tamale 160
    Stuffed Beef Rolls 210
    Tamale Pie 96
One-Pot Pasta 38
onions
    Bacon Burgers 19
    Baked Beef & Potato Layers 107
    Basic Ground Beef Mix 10

Battered Beef 44
Béchamel Lasagna 70
Beef & Cheese Cobbler 120
Beef & Cheese Roll 131
Beef & Noodles 26
Beef & Pine Nut Triangles 191
Beef & Potato Rissoles 49
Beef & Tomato Soup 14
Beef & Vegetable Gratin 137
Beef & Wild Rice 194
Beef Curry 172
Beef Fried Rice 28
Beef in Pita Pockets 84
Beef Keftas 20
Beef 'n' Beans 87
Beef Pilaf 197
Beef Potpie 119
Beef Roulade 215
Beef Samosas 177
Beef Tamale 160
Beef with Bell Pepper, Fruit & Nuts 209
Beef with Garlic Potatoes 101
Beef with Pimientos 110
Beef with Scrambled Eggs 22
Beef-Filled Crêpes 116
Bolognese Soufflé 126
Braised Hamburgers 104
Burritos 153
Cheese-Stuffed Hamburgers 75
Chili con Carne 148
Chinese Soup with Meatballs 186
Crispy Beef Fritters 37
Curry Puffs 168
Dutch Crêpe Cake 134
Eggplant Rolls 216
Empanadas 154
Enchiladas 147
Fiery Beef Tacos 150
French Beef Patties in Red Wine 203
French Meat Tart 122
Fried Beef Dumplings 114
Greek Baked Pasta 125
Ground Beef & Mashed Vegetables 78
Ground Beef Hash 88
Ground Beef Pizza 82
Ground Beef Stroganoff 212
Ground Beef with Potato Topping 98
Hamburgers with Beet 128
Homemade Hamburgers 16
Indian Kabobs 171
Indian Potato Cakes 174
Lasagna 40
Layered Beef & Feta 108
Lemon Beef in Walnut Sauce 206
Meat Loaf 63
Meatball Goulash 183
Meatballs 58
Meaty Macaroni & Cheese 66
Meaty Muffins 55
Mexican Beef Stew 159
Nachos 156
One-Pot Pasta 38
Puff Pastry Meat Loaf 198
Quick Curry 31
Russian Beef & Onion Pastries 192
Salisbury Casserole 113
Salisbury Steak 93
Savory Croquettes 46
Simple Savory Beef 90
Sloppy Joes 72
Spaghetti & Meatballs 69
Spaghetti Bolognese 64
Spiced Beef & Pistachios 178
Spicy Beef & Sweet Potatoes 162
Spicy Ground Beef Casserole 165
Stuffed Baked Potatoes 81
Stuffed Beef Rolls 210
Stuffed Bell Peppers 76
Stuffed Onions 52
Swedish Meatballs 60
Taco Soup 142
Tamale Pie 96
Tex-Mex Pizza 34
see also scallions; shallots

paprika
    Beef Keftas 20
    Beef with Pimientos 110
    Burritos 153

Ground Beef Hash 88
Hamburgers with Beef 128
Meatball Goulash 183
Savory Croquettes 46
Parmesan cheese
   Béchamel Lasagna 70
   Beef & Spinach Cannelloni 138
   Bolognese Soufflé 126
   Enchiladas 147
   Greek Baked Pasta 125
   Italian Croquettes 200
   Layered Beef & Feta 108
parsley
   Battered Beef 44
   Béchamel Lasagna 70
   Beef & Cheese Roll 131
   Beef & Potato Rissoles 49
   Beef & Tomato Soup 14
   Beef & Vegetable Gratin 137
   Beef Roulade 215
   Beef with Garlic Potatoes 101
   Beef with Scrambled Eggs 22
   Crispy Beef Fritters 37
   Dutch Crêpe Cake 134
   French Beef Patties in Red Wine 203
   Glazed Beef 218
   Greek Baked Pasta 125
   Ground Beef Hash 88
   Ground Beef Stroganoff 212
   Homemade Hamburgers 16
   Italian Croquettes 200
   Lasagna 40
   Meat Loaf 63
   Meaty Muffins 55
   One-Pot Pasta 38
   Pasta Shells with Aromatic Beef Sauce 180
   Puff Pastry Meat Loaf 198
   Savory Croquettes 46
   Spicy Ground Beef Casserole 165
   Stuffed Beef Rolls 210
parsnips: Ground Beef & Mashed Vegetables 78
pasta
   Béchamel Lasagna 70
   Beef & Spinach Cannelloni 138
   Bolognese Soufflé 126
   Greek Baked Pasta 125
   Lasagna 40
   Meaty Macaroni & Cheese 66
   One-Pot Pasta 38
   Pasta Shells with Aromatic Beef Sauce 180
   Spaghetti & Meatballs 69
   Spaghetti Bolognese 64
pastry
   Beef & Pine Nut Triangles 191
   Beef Potpie 119
   Beef Samosas 177
   Curry Puffs 168
   Eggplant Rolls 216
   Empanadas 154
   French Meat Tart 122
   Indonesian Beef Parcels 166
   Puff Pastry Meat Loaf 198
   Russian Beef & Onion Pastries 192
peas
   Beef Fried Rice 28
   Curry Puffs 168
   Indian Potato Cakes 174
   Simple Savory Beef 90
pimientos: Beef with Pimientos 110
pine nuts
   Beef & Pine Nut Triangles 191
   Beef in Pita Pockets 84
pineapple: Ground Beef Casserole 102
pita breads: Beef in Pita Pockets 84
pizzas
   Ground Beef Pizza 82
   Tex-Mex Pizza 34
potatoes
   Baked Beef & Potato Layers 107
   Beef & Pine Nut Triangles 191
   Beef & Potato Rissoles 49
   Beef & Tomato Soup 14
   Beef 'n' Beans 87
   Beef with Garlic Potatoes 101
   Beefy Baked Potatoes 43
   Ground Beef & Mashed Vegetables 78
   Ground Beef Hash 88
   Ground Beef with Potato Topping 98
   Indian Potato Cakes 174

Layered Beef & Feta 108
Meatball Goulash 183
Stuffed Baked Potatoes 81
Swedish Meatballs 60
pumpkin: Beef & Pumpkin Baked with Rice 204

Quick Curry 31

raisins & golden raisins
   Beef & Vegetable Gratin 137
   Beef Tamale 160
   Empanadas 154
   Spicy Ground Beef Casserole 165
   Stuffed Bell Peppers 76
red wine
   Beef Potpie 119
   Burritos 153
   French Beef Patties in Red Wine 203
   Meatball Goulash 183
   One-Pot Pasta 38
   Pasta Shells with Aromatic Beef Sauce 180
refried beans
   Nachos 156
   Tex-Mex Pizza 34
rice
   Beef & Pumpkin Baked with Rice 204
   Beef & Wild Rice 194
   Beef Fried Rice 28
   Beef Pilaf 197
   Beef Soup with Ginger & Lemongrass 188
   Italian Croquettes 200
   Meal-in-a-Bowl Beef & Herb Soup 132
   Russian Beef & Onion Pastries 192
Rissoles 49
Russian Beef & Onion Pastries 192

sage
   Bacon Burgers 19
   Beef with Garlic Potatoes 101
   Cabbage Rolls 50
   French Meat Tart 122
   Stuffed Baked Potatoes 81
Salisbury Casserole 113
Salisbury Steak 93
sausage: French Meat Tart 122
Savory Croquettes 46
scallions
   Beef Soup with Ginger & Lemongrass 188
   Beefy Baked Potatoes 43
   Cabbage Rolls 50
   Chinese Noodles with Beef & Shredded Vegetables 221
   Chinese Soup with Meatballs 186
   Fiery Beef Tacos 150
   Ground Beef Casserole 102
   Stir-Fried Beef 25
   Thai Beef Omelet 32
shallots
   Beef & Spinach Cannelloni 138
   Beef Soup with Ginger & Lemongrass 188
   Braised Hamburgers 104
   Glazed Beef 218
   Indonesian Beef Parcels 166
   Italian Croquettes 200
   Pasta Shells with Aromatic Beef Sauce 180
   Stuffed Beef Rolls 210
Simple Savory Beef 90
Sloppy Joes 72
snow peas: Beef & Noodles 26
soups
   Beef & Tomato Soup 14
   Beef Soup with Ginger & Lemongrass 188
   Chinese Soup with Meatballs 186
   Meal-in-a-Bowl Beef & Herb Soup 132
   Taco Soup 142
sour cream
   Fiery Beef Tacos 150
   Ground Beef Stroganoff 212
   Hamburgers with Beef 128
   Meatball Goulash 183
   Nachos 156
   Russian Beef & Onion Pastries 192
   Savory Croquettes 46
   Spiced Beef & Pistachios 178
   Taco Soup 142
   Tamale Pie 96
Spaghetti & Meatballs 69
Spaghetti Bolognese 64
Spiced Beef & Pistachios 178

Spicy Beef & Sweet Potatoes 162
Spicy Ground Beef Casserole 165
spinach
   Beef & Spinach Cannelloni 138
   Meal-in-a-Bowl Beef & Herb Soup 132
split peas: Meal-in-a-Bowl Beef & Herb Soup 132
Stir-Fried Beef 25
Stuffed Baked Potatoes 81
Stuffed Beef Rolls 210
Stuffed Bell Peppers 76
Stuffed Onions 52
Swedish Meatballs 60
sweet potatoes: Spicy Beef & Sweet Potatoes 162

taco shells: Fiery Beef Tacos 150
Taco Soup 142
Tamale Pie 96
Tex-Mex Pizza 34
Thai Beef Omelet 32
thyme
   Baked Beef & Potato Layers 107
   Beef & Cheese Cobbler 120
   Beef Tamale 160
   Bolognese Soufflé 126
   Cheese-Stuffed Hamburgers 75
   Glazed Beef 218
   Ground Beef & Mashed Vegetables 78
   Ground Beef Casserole 102
   Spaghetti & Meatballs 69
   Stuffed Baked Potatoes 81
tomatoes
   Baked Beef & Potato Layers 107
   Béchamel Lasagna 70
   Beef & Spinach Cannelloni 138
   Beef & Tomato Soup 14
   Beef Curry 172
   Beef in Pita Pockets 84
   Beef Potpie 119
   Beef with Bell Pepper, Fruit & Nuts 209
   Beef with Garlic Potatoes 101
   Beef with Scrambled Eggs 22
   Bolognese Soufflé 126
   Burritos 153
   Cabbage Rolls 50
   Chili con Carne 148
   Curry Puffs 168
   Eggplant Rolls 216
   Empanadas 154
   Enchiladas 147
   Fiery Beef Tacos 150
   Greek Baked Pasta 125
   Ground Beef Casserole 102
   Lasagna 40
   Layered Beef & Feta 108
   Meatballs 58
   Meaty Macaroni & Cheese 66
   One-Pot Pasta 38
   Pasta Shells with Aromatic Beef Sauce 180
   Quick Curry 31
   Simple Savory Beef 90
   Spaghetti & Meatballs 69
   Spaghetti Bolognese 64
   Spiced Beef & Pistachios 178
   Spicy Beef & Sweet Potatoes 162
   Stuffed Baked Potatoes 81
   Stuffed Beef Rolls 210
   Taco Soup 142
   Tamale Pie 96
   Thai Beef Omelet 32
top round steak
   Beef Roulade 215
   Stuffed Beef Rolls 210
tortilla chips
   Nachos 156
   Taco Soup 142
tortillas
   Burritos 153
   Enchiladas 147

watercress: Chinese Soup with Meatballs 186

yogurt
   Beef Keftas 20
   Indian Kabobs 171
   Layered Beef & Feta 108

zucchini: Beef & Vegetable Gratin 137